PRAYERS TO START YOUR DAY

BY CRISWELL FREEMAN

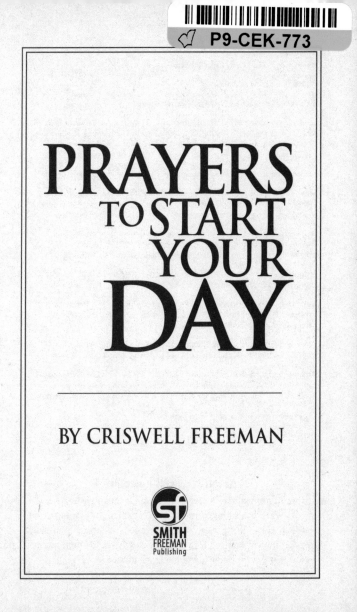

SMITH FREEMAN
Publishing

Prayers to Start Your Day by Criswell Freeman

©2019 Smith Freeman Publishing

Bible verses were taken from the following translations:

Scripture quotations marked HCSB® are taken from the Holman Christian Standard Bible®, Copyright © 1999, 2000, 2002, 2003, 2009 by Holman Bible Publishers. Used by permission. HCSB®' is a federally registered trademark of Holman Bible Publishers.

Scripture quotations marked KJV are from the King James Version. Public domain.

Scripture quotations marked MSG are taken from *THE MESSAGE*, copyright © 1993, 1994, 1995, 1996, 2000, 2001, 2002 by Eugene H. Peterson. Used by permission of NavPress. All rights reserved. Represented by Tyndal House Publishers, Inc.

Scripture quotations marked NASB are from the New American Standard Bible® (NASB), Copyright © 1960, 1962, 1963,1968, 1971, 1972, 1973, 1975, 1977, 1995 by the Lockman Foundation. Used by permission. www.Lockman.org.

Scripture quotations marked NCV are from the New Century Version®. Copyright © 2005 by Thomas Nelson. Used by permission. All rights reserved.

Scripture quotations marked NIV are from The Holy Bible, New International Version® NIV® copyright © 1973, 1978, 1984, 2011 by Biblica, Inc. Used by permission. All rights reserved worldwide.

Scripture quotations marked NKJV are from the New King James Version®. Copyright © 1982 by Thomas Nelson. Used by permission. All rights reserved.

Scripture quotations marked NLT are from the *Holy Bible*, New Living Translation, copyright © 1996, 2004, 2015 by Tyndale House Foundation. Used by permission of Tyndale House Publishers, Inc., Carol Stream, Illinois 60188. All rights reserved.

Cover design by Kim Russell | Wahoo Designs

ISBN: 978-0-9997706-5-8

About Criswell Freeman

Criswell Freeman is a Doctor of Clinical Psychology who, over the last 25 years, has authored numerous Christian, inspirational, and self-help titles. With over 20 million books in print, he usually avoids publicity and prefers to work quietly—and often anonymously—from his home in Nashville, Tennessee.

A Message to Readers

Each day provides opportunities to put God where He belongs: at the center of our lives. When we do so, we worship Him, not only with our words and deeds, but also with our prayers.

This text contains one hundred devotional readings that are intended to remind you of the eternal promises that are found in God's holy Word. On these pages, you'll be reminded of the need for prayer and the power of prayer. If you're already committed to a regular morning devotional, this book will enrich that experience. If you are not, the simple act of giving God a few minutes each day will change the direction and the quality of your life.

Today and every day, keep searching for direction—God's direction. And while you're at it, keep searching for perspective and wisdom—starting with God's wisdom. When you do, you'll discover the comfort, the power, and the peace that can be yours when you start each day with prayer.

1

Begin Your Day with God

He awakens Me morning by morning, He awakens My ear
to hear as the learned. The Lord GOD has opened My ear.

ISAIAH 50:4–5 NKJV

Want to worry less and enjoy life more? If so, here's a simple prescription that's tested and true: spend time with God every morning.

Each new day is a gift from God, and if we are wise, we spend a few quiet moments each morning thanking the Giver. When we begin each day with heads bowed and hearts lifted, we remind ourselves of God's love, His protection, and His commandments. And we can align our priorities for the coming day with the teachings and commandments that God has given us through His holy Word.

Are you seeking to change some aspect of your life? If so, ask for God's help and ask for it many times each day, starting with your morning devotional.

Begin each day with God. It will change your priorities.

ELIZABETH GEORGE

A Prayer to Start Your Day

Dear Lord, every day of my life is a journey with You. I will take time today to think, to pray, and to study Your Word. Guide my steps, Father, and keep me mindful that today offers yet another opportunity to celebrate Your blessings, Your love, and Your Son. Amen.

2
Study His Word

You will be a good servant of Christ Jesus, nourished by the words of the faith and of the good teaching that you have followed.

1 TIMOTHY 4:6 HCSB

God's Word is unlike any other book. The Bible is a roadmap for life here on earth and for life eternal. As Christians, we are called upon to study God's Holy Word, to trust its promises, to follow its commandments, and to share its Good News with the world.

As believers who seek to follow in the footsteps of the One from Galilee, we must study the Bible and meditate upon its meaning for our lives. Otherwise we deprive ourselves of a priceless gift from our Creator. God's holy Word is, indeed, a transforming, life-changing, one-of-a-kind treasure. A passing acquaintance with the Good Book is insufficient for Christians who seek to obey God's Word and to understand His will.

The Scriptures were not given to increase our knowledge but to change our lives.

D. L. MOODY

A Prayer to Start Your Day

Dear Lord, the Bible is Your gift to me; let me use it. When I place Your Word at the very center of my life, I am blessed. Make me a faithful student of Your Word so that I might be a faithful servant in Your world, this day and every day. Amen.

3

Entrust Your Hopes to God

You, LORD, give true peace to those who
depend on you, because they trust you.
ISAIAH 26:3 NCV

Hope is a perishable commodity. Despite God's promises, despite Christ's love, and despite our countless blessings, we frail human beings can still lose hope from time to time. When we do, we need the encouragement of Christian friends, the life-changing power of prayer, and the healing truth of God's holy Word.

The Bible teaches that the Lord blesses those who trust in His wisdom and follow in the footsteps of His Son. Will you count yourself among that number? When you do, you'll have every reason on earth—and in heaven—to be hopeful about your future. After all, God has made important promises to you, promises that He is certainly going to keep. So be hopeful, be optimistic, be faithful, and do your best. Then, leave the rest up to God. Your destiny is safe with Him.

Never yield to gloomy anticipation. Place your hope
and confidence in God. He has no record of failure.
LETTIE COWMAN

A Prayer to Start Your Day

Dear Lord, I will place my hope in You. If I become discouraged, I will turn to You. If I am afraid, I will seek strength in You. In every aspect of my life, I will trust You. You are my Father, and I will place my hope, my trust, and my faith in You. Amen.

4

Perseverance Pays

But thanks be to God, who gives us the victory through our Lord Jesus Christ. Therefore, my beloved brethren, be steadfast, immovable, always abounding in the work of the Lord, knowing that your labor is not in vain in the Lord.

1 Corinthians 15:57–58 NKJV

A well-lived life is like a marathon, not a sprint—it calls for preparation, determination, and, of course, lots of perseverance. As an example of perfect perseverance, we Christians need look no further than Jesus Christ.

Jesus finished what He began. Despite His suffering and despite the unspeakable pain He experienced on the cross, Jesus was steadfast in His faithfulness to God. We, too, must remain faithful when we experience the inevitable hardships of life.

Are you living through tough times or facing a difficult situation? If so, just keep putting one foot in front of the other, pray for strength, and keep going. Whatever your problem, God can handle it. Your job is to keep persevering until He does.

Perseverance is more than endurance. It is endurance combined with absolute assurance and certainty that what we are looking for is going to happen.

Oswald Chambers

A Prayer to Start Your Day

Lord, when life is difficult, I am tempted to abandon hope in the future. But You are my God, and I can draw strength from You. Let me trust You, Father, in good times and in trying times. Let me persevere—even if my soul is troubled—and let me follow Your Son this day and forever. Amen.

5

Pray for Perspective

*All I'm doing right now, friends, is showing how these things
pertain to Apollos and me so that you will learn restraint and not
rush into making judgments without knowing all the facts.
It's important to look at things from God's point of view.*

1 CORINTHIANS 4:6 MSG

If a temporary loss of perspective has left you worried, exhausted, or both, it's time to readjust your thought patterns. Negative thoughts are habit-forming; thankfully, so are positive ones. With practice, you can form the habit of focusing on God's priorities and your own possibilities. When you do, you'll soon discover that you will spend less time fretting about your challenges and more time praising God for His gifts.

When you call upon the Lord and prayerfully seek His will, He will give you wisdom and perspective. When you make God's priorities your priorities, He will direct your steps and calm your fears. So today and every day hereafter, pray for a sense of balance and perspective. And remember: no problems are too big for God—and that includes yours.

*Instead of being frustrated and overwhelmed by all that is going on
in our world, go to the Lord and ask Him to give you His eternal perspective.*
KAY ARTHUR

A Prayer to Start Your Day

Dear Lord, give me wisdom and perspective. Guide me according to Your plans for my life and according to Your commandments. And keep me mindful, dear Lord, and that Your truth is—and will forever be—the ultimate truth. Amen.

6

Be a Joyful Christian

Make me hear joy and gladness.
PSALM 51:8 NKJV

The joy that the world offers is fleeting and incomplete: here today, gone tomorrow, not coming back anytime soon. But God's joy is different. His joy has staying power. In fact, it's a gift that never stops giving to those who welcome His Son into their hearts.

Sometimes, amid the inevitable complications and predicaments that are woven into the fabric of everyday life, we forget to rejoice. Instead of celebrating life, we complain about it. This is an understandable mistake, but a mistake nonetheless. As Christians, we are called by our Creator to live joyfully and abundantly. To do otherwise is to squander His spiritual gifts.

This day and every day, Christ offers you His peace and His joy. Accept it and share it with others, just as He has shared His joy with you.

Joy is the serious business of heaven.
C. S. LEWIS

A Prayer to Start Your Day

Dear Lord, You have given me so many blessings, starting with my family. I will keep joy in my heart as I thank You, Lord, for every single blessing You've given me. Amen.

Forgive Everybody

For if you forgive people their wrongdoing, your heavenly Father
will forgive you as well. But if you don't forgive people,
your Father will not forgive your wrongdoing.
MATTHEW 6:14–15 HCSB

The world holds few if any rewards for those who remain angrily focused upon the past. Still, the act of forgiveness is difficult for all but the most saintly Christian. Are you mired in the quicksand of bitterness or regret? If so, you are not only disobeying God's Word, you are also wasting your time.

Being frail, fallible, imperfect human beings, most of us are quick to anger, quick to blame, slow to forgive, and even slower to forget. Yet as Christians, we are commanded to forgive others, just as we, too, have been forgiven.

If there exists even one person—alive or dead—against whom you hold bitter feelings, it's time to forgive. Or, if you are embittered against yourself for some past mistake or shortcoming, it's finally time to forgive yourself and move on. Hatred, bitterness, and regret are not part of God's plan for your life. Forgiveness is.

Remember that you will never be spiritually blessed until you forgive.
NORMAN VINCENT PEALE

A Prayer to Start Your Day

Dear Lord, let forgiveness rule my heart, even when forgiveness is difficult. Let me be Your obedient servant, Lord, and let me forgive others just as You have forgiven me. Amen.

Follow Your Conscience

Let us draw near with a true heart in full assurance of faith,
our hearts sprinkled clean from an evil conscience
and our bodies washed in pure water.
HEBREWS 10:22 HCSB

God has given each of us a conscience, and He intends for us to use it. But sometimes we don't. Instead of listening to that quiet inner voice that warns us against disobedience and danger, we're tempted to rush headlong into situations that we soon come to regret.

God promises that He rewards good conduct and that He blesses those who obey His Word. The Lord also issues a stern warning to those who rebel against His commandments. Wise Christians heed that warning. Count yourself among their number.

Sometime soon, perhaps today, your conscience will speak; when it does, listen carefully. God may be trying to get a message through to you. And it may be a message you desperately need to hear.

Conscience is our wisest counselor and teacher,
our most faithful and most patient friend.
BILLY GRAHAM

A Prayer to Start Your Day

Dear Lord, You speak to me through that still, small voice that tells me what to do. That voice warns me when I stray from Your will. In these quiet moments and throughout the day, show me Your plan for my life, Lord, that I might serve You. Amen.

9

Experience God's Grace

For by grace you have been saved through faith,
and that not of yourselves; it is the gift of God.
EPHESIANS 2:8 NKJV

God's grace is not earned. Thank goodness! To earn God's love and His gift of eternal life would be far beyond the abilities of even the most righteous man or woman. Thankfully, grace is not an earthly reward for righteous behavior; it is a blessed spiritual gift, which can be accepted by believers who dedicate themselves to God through Christ. When we accept Christ into our hearts, we are saved by His grace.

The familiar words of Ephesians 2:8 make God's promise perfectly clear: it is by grace we have been saved, through faith.

God's grace is the ultimate gift, and we owe to Him the ultimate in thanksgiving. Let us praise the Creator for His priceless gift, and let us share the Good News with all who cross our paths. We return our Father's love by accepting His grace and by sharing His message and His love.

God is the giver, and we are the receivers. And His richest gifts are
bestowed not upon those who do the greatest things, but upon those
who accept His abundance and His grace.
HANNAH WHITALL SMITH

A Prayer to Start Your Day

Dear Lord, I have fallen short of Your commandments, and You have forgiven me. You have blessed me with Your love and Your mercy. Enable me to be merciful toward others, Father, just as You have been merciful to me, and let me share Your love with everyone I meet. Amen.

10

Pray More, Worry Less

Don't worry about anything, but in everything, through prayer and petition with thanksgiving, let your requests be made known to God.
PHILIPPIANS 4:6 HCSB

If you are like most people, it is simply a fact of life: from time to time, you worry. You worry about health, about finances, about safety, about relationships, about family, and about an assortment of obligations, some great and some small. Where is the best place to take your worries? Take them to God. Take your troubles to Him, and your fears, and your sorrows.

Barbara Johnson correctly observed, "Worry is the senseless process of cluttering up tomorrow's opportunities with leftover problems from today." So if you'd like to make the most out of this day (and every one hereafter), turn your worries over to a Power greater than yourself—and spend your valuable time and energy solving the problems you can fix while trusting God to do the rest.

Replace worry with prayer. Make the decision to pray whenever you catch yourself worrying.
ELIZABETH GEORGE

A Prayer to Start Your Day

Dear Lord, wherever I find myself, let me celebrate more and worry less. When my faith begins to waver, help me to trust You more. Then, with praise on my lips and the love of Your Son in my heart, let me live courageously, faithfully, prayerfully, and thankfully this day and every day. Amen.

11

Put God in His Rightful Place: First Place

Do not have other gods besides Me.
EXODUS 20:3 HCSB

As you think about the nature of your relationship with God, remember this: You will always have some type of relationship with Him—it is inevitable that your life must be lived in relationship to God. The question is not if you will have a relationship with Him; the burning question is whether that relationship will be one that seeks to honor Him . . . or not.

Are you willing to place God first in your life? And are you willing to welcome Him into your heart? Unless you can honestly answer these questions with a resounding yes, you'll constantly be worrying about things that are better left up to Him.

Be thankful that God is always available; He's always ready to listen; and, He's waiting to hear from you now. The rest, of course, is up to you.

*The most important thing you must decide
to do every day is put the Lord first.*
ELIZABETH GEORGE

A Prayer to Start Your Day

Dear Lord, Your love is eternal and Your laws are everlasting. Today I invite You to reign over every corner of my heart. I will have faith in You, Father. I will sense Your presence; I will accept Your love; I will trust Your will; and I will praise You for the Savior of my life: Your Son Jesus. Amen.

12

Keep Searching for Wisdom

*Now if any of you lacks wisdom, he should ask God,
who gives to all generously and without criticizing, and it will be
given to him. But let him ask in faith without doubting. For the
doubter is like the surging sea, driven and tossed by the wind.*

JAMES 1:5–6 HCSB

Where will you find wisdom today? Will you seek it from God or from the world? As a thoughtful believer living in a society that is filled with temptations and distractions, you know that the world's brand of "wisdom" is everywhere, and it is dangerous. You live in a world where it's all too easy to stray far from the ultimate source of wisdom: God's holy Word.

In theory, all of us would prefer to be wise, but not all of us are willing to make the sacrifices that are required to gain real wisdom. To become wise, we must do more than spout platitudes, recite verses, or repeat aphorisms. We must not only speak wisely; we must live wisely. We must not only learn the lessons of the Christian life; we must live by them.

Today, as you prepare yourself for the inevitable ups and downs of everyday life, remember that God's wisdom can be found in a book that's already on your bookshelf: His Book. Read, heed, and live accordingly.

A Prayer to Start Your Day

Lord, make me a person of wisdom and discernment. I seek wisdom, Lord, not as the world gives, but as You give. Lead me in Your ways and teach me from Your Word so that, in time, my wisdom might glorify Your kingdom and Your Son. Amen.

13

Do First Things First

So prepare your minds for action and exercise self-control.
1 PETER 1:13 NLT

First things first." These words are easy to speak but hard to put into practice. If you're having trouble prioritizing your day, perhaps you've been trying to organize your life according to your own plans, not God's. A better strategy, of course, is to take your daily obligations and place them in the hands of the One who created you. To do so, you must prioritize your day according to God's commandments, and you must seek His will and His wisdom in all matters. Then, you can face the day with the assurance that the same God who created our universe out of nothingness will help you place first things first in your own life.

Do you feel anxious, overwhelmed, or confused? If so, turn the concerns of this day over to God—prayerfully, earnestly, and often. Then listen for His answer, and trust the answer He gives.

Put first things first and we get second things thrown in; put second things first and we lose both first and second things.
ELIZABETH GEORGE

A Prayer to Start Your Day

Dear Lord, today is a new day. Help me finish the important tasks first, even if those tasks are unpleasant. Don't let me put off until tomorrow what I should do today. Amen.

14

Trust Him
When Times Are Tough

Praise the God and Father of our Lord Jesus Christ, the Father of mercies and the God of all comfort. He comforts us in all our affliction, so that we may be able to comfort those who are in any kind of affliction, through the comfort we ourselves receive from God.

2 Corinthians 1:3–4 HCSB

The Bible promises this: Tough times are temporary but God's love is not. God's love lasts forever. So what does that mean to you? Just this: from time to time, everybody faces tough times, and so will you. And when tough times arrive, God will always stand ready to protect you and heal you.

Psalm 147:3 promises, "He heals the brokenhearted" (NIV), but it doesn't say that He heals them instantly. Usually, it takes time for God to fix things. So if you're facing tough times, face them with God by your side. If you find yourself in any kind of trouble, pray about it and ask God for help. And be patient. God will work things out, just as He has promised, but He will do it in His own way and in His own time.

Measure the size of the obstacles against the size of God.

Beth Moore

A Prayer to Start Your Day

Dear heavenly Father, You are my strength and my protector. When I am troubled, You comfort me. When I am discouraged, You lift me up. Your love is infinite, as is Your wisdom. Whatever my circumstances, dear Lord, let me always give the praise, and the thanks, and the glory to You. Amen.

15

The World Changes, But God Does Not

There is a time for everything,
and a season for every activity under the heavens.
ECCLESIASTES 3:1 NIV

Our world is in a state of constant change. God is not. At times, the world seems to be trembling beneath our feet. But we can be comforted in the knowledge that our heavenly Father is the rock that cannot be shaken. His Word promises, "I am the LORD, I do not change" (Malachi 3:6 NKJV).

We mortals encounter a multitude of changes—some good, some not so good. And on occasion, all of us must endure life-changing personal losses that leave us breathless. When we do, our loving heavenly Father stands ready to protect us, to comfort us, to guide us, and, in time, to heal us.

Are you facing difficult circumstances? Please remember that God is far bigger than any problem you may face. And it is because the Lord does not change that you can face your challenges with courage for this day and hope for the future.

Conditions are always changing; therefore, I must not
be dependent upon conditions. What matters
supremely is my soul and my relationship to God.
CORRIE TEN BOOM

A Prayer to Start Your Day

Dear Lord, our world is constantly changing. When I face the inevitable transitions of life, I will turn to You for strength and assurance. Thank You, Father, for love that is unchanging and everlasting. Amen.

16

Be Enthusiastic

Don't work only while being watched, in order to please men,
but as slaves of Christ, do God's will from your heart.
Serve with a good attitude, as to the Lord and not to men.
EPHESIANS 6:6-7 HCSB

If you'd like to worry less, try celebrating more. And when you think about it, celebrating shouldn't be very hard because each day has its own share of blessings. Our assignment, as grateful believers, is to look for the blessings and celebrate them.

Today, like every other day, is a priceless gift from God. He has offered us yet another opportunity to serve Him with smiling faces and willing hands. When we do our part, He inevitably does His part, and miracles happen.

The Lord has promised to bless you and keep you, now and forever. So don't wait for birthdays or holidays. Make this day an exciting adventure. And while you're at it, take time to thank God for His blessings. He deserves your gratitude, and you deserve the joy of expressing it.

Enthusiasm, like the flu, is contagious—we get it from one another.
BARBARA JOHNSON

A Prayer to Start Your Day

Dear Lord, I know that others are watching the way that I live my life. Help me to be an enthusiastic Christian with a faith that is contagious. Amen.

17

Listen Carefully to Your Creator

The one who is from God listens to God's words.
JOHN 8:47 HCSB

As you search for solutions to the inevitable challenges of everyday life, be sure to talk often with your heavenly Father. And after you've finished talking, listen carefully, as God speaks to us in different ways at different times. Sometimes He speaks loudly and clearly. But more often, He speaks in a quiet voice that's best heard in silence. So you must carve out quiet moments each day to study His Word and to sense His direction.

Are you willing to pray sincerely and then to wait patiently for God's response? Are you attuned to the subtle guidance of your intuition? I hope so. Usually God refrains from sending His messages on stone tablets or city billboards. More often, He communicates in subtler ways. If you sincerely desire to hear His voice, you must listen carefully, and you must do so in the silent corners of your quiet, willing heart.

When God speaks, oftentimes His voice
will call for an act of courage on our part.
CHARLES STANLEY

A Prayer to Start Your Day

Lord, give me the wisdom to be a good listener. Help me listen carefully to my family, to my friends, and—most importantly— to You. Amen.

18

Trust God's Promises

For you need endurance, so that after you have done God's will,
you may receive what was promised.

HEBREWS 10:36 HCSB

God's promises are found in a book like no other: the Holy Bible. The Bible is a roadmap for life here on earth and for life eternal. As Christians, we are called upon to trust its promises, to follow its commandments, and to share its Good News.

If we wish to be faithful disciples of Christ, we must study the Bible daily and meditate upon its meaning for our lives. Otherwise we deprive ourselves of a priceless gift from our Creator. God's holy Word is, indeed, a transforming, life-changing, one-of-a-kind treasure. And a passing acquaintance with the Good Book is insufficient for Christians who seek to obey God's Word and to understand His will.

As we face the inevitable worries and obligations of life here on earth, we must arm ourselves with the promises of God's holy Word. When we do, we can expect the best, not only for the day ahead, but also for all eternity.

God's promises can never fail to be accomplished,
and those who patiently wait can never be disappointed,
for a believing faith leads to realization.

LETTIE COWMAN

A Prayer to Start Your Day

Lord, Your holy Word contains promises, and I will trust them. I will use the Bible as my guide, and I will trust You, Lord, to speak to me through Your Holy Spirit and through Your holy Word, this day and forever. Amen.

19

Return God's Love by Sharing It

Dear friends, if God loved us in this way,
we also must love one another.
1 JOHN 4:11 HCSB

Sometimes, amid the crush of everyday life, God may seem very far away. He is not. The Lord is always with us, night and day; He never leaves us, even for a moment.

God loves you so much that He sent His Son to die for you. Now, precisely because you are a wondrous creation treasured by God, a question presents itself: What will you do in response to God's love? Will you ignore it or embrace it? Will you return it or neglect it? The decision, of course, is yours and yours alone.

When you embrace God's love, you are transformed. When you embrace God's love, you feel differently about yourself, your neighbors, and your world. When you embrace God's love, you can keep your problems in perspective because you know that every earthly inconvenience is temporary but that God's love is eternal.

There is no limit to God. There is no limit to His power.
There is no limit to His love. There is no limit to His mercy.
BILLY GRAHAM

A Prayer to Start Your Day

Dear God, You are love. You love me, Father, and I love You. As I love You more, Lord, I am also able to love my family and friends more. I will be Your loving servant, heavenly Father, today and throughout eternity. Amen.

20

When You Have Doubts, Pray

*Now if any of you lacks wisdom, he should ask God, who gives
to all generously and without criticizing, and it will be given to him.
But let him ask in faith without doubting. For the doubter
is like the surging sea, driven and tossed by the wind.*

JAMES 1:5–6 HCSB

If you've never had any doubts about your faith, then you can stop reading this page now and skip to the next. But if you've ever been plagued by doubts about your faith or your Creator, keep reading.

Even some of the most faithful Christians are, at times, beset by occasional bouts of discouragement and doubt. But even when we feel far removed from God, God is never far removed from us. He is always with us, always willing to calm the storms of life—always willing to replace our doubts with comfort and assurance.

Whenever you're plagued by doubts, that's precisely the moment you should seek God's presence by genuinely seeking to establish a deeper, more meaningful relationship with His Son. Then you may rest assured that in time, God will calm your fears, answer your prayers, and restore your confidence.

A Prayer to Start Your Day

Dear God, sometimes this world can be a puzzling place, filled with uncertainty and doubt. When I am unsure of my next step, keep me mindful that You are always near and that You can overcome any challenge. Give me faith, Father, so that I can live courageously and faithfully today and every day. Amen.

21

Let God Guide You during Difficult Days

*We also have joy with our troubles, because we know
that these troubles produce patience. And patience
produces character, and character produces hope.*

ROMANS 5:3-4 NCV

All days are not created equal. Some days are bright and cheery while other days are decidedly darker. When tough times arise, as they inevitably do from time to time, we are tempted to complain, to worry, and to do little else. A far better strategy, of course, is to pray more, to worry less, and to get busy addressing our problems.

Sometimes even the most optimistic believers can become discouraged, and you are no exception. So if you find yourself enduring difficult circumstances, remember that God remains in His heaven. And if you become discouraged with the direction of your day or your life, lift your thoughts and prayers to Him. He is a God of possibility, not negativity. He will guide you through your difficulties and beyond them. Then you can thank the Giver of all things good for blessings that are simply too numerous to count.

A Prayer to Start Your Day

Dear Lord, when the day is difficult, give me perspective and faith. When I am weak, give me strength. Let me trust in Your promises, Father, and let me live with the assurance that You are with me not only today but also throughout all eternity. Amen.

22

You Have a Very Bright Future

When problems arise, as they do from time to time, the future may seem foreboding. But if you take your troubles to the Lord and leave them there, your future is secure because God's promises are true.

Are you willing to place your future in the hands of a loving and all-knowing Creator? Will you face today's challenges with hope and optimism? You should. After all, God created you for a very important purpose: His purpose. And you have important work to do: His work. So today, as you live in the present and look to the future, remember that God has a marvelous plan for you.

A Prayer to Start Your Day

Dear Lord, as I look to the future, I will place my trust in You. If I become discouraged, I will turn to You. If I am afraid, I will seek strength in You. You are my Father, and I will place my hope, my trust, and my faith in You. Amen.

23

Be Still

Be still, and know that I am God.
PSALM 46:10 NKJV

We live in a noisy world, a world filled with distractions, frustrations, and complications. But if we allow the distractions of a clamorous world to separate us from God's peace, we do ourselves a profound disservice.

Do you rush through the day with scarcely a single moment for quiet contemplation and prayer? If so, it's time to reorder your priorities. Nothing is more important than the quiet moments you spend with your Creator. So be still and claim the peace that is your spiritual birthright. It is offered freely; it has been paid for in full; it is yours for the asking. So ask. And then share.

A Prayer to Start Your Day

Lord, Your holy Word is a light unto the world; help me be still so I can study it, trust it, and share it with all who cross my path. Help me to be a worthy witness as I share the Good News of Your perfect Son and Your perfect Word. Amen.

24

Give God Your Full Attention

Who is in charge of your heart? Is it God, or is it something else? Have you given Christ your heart, your soul, your talents, your time, and your testimony? Or are you giving Him little more than a few hours each Sunday morning?

In the book of Exodus, God warns that we should place no gods before Him. Yet all too often, we place our Lord in second, third, or fourth place as we worship other things. When we unwittingly place possessions or relationships above our love for the Creator, we create big problems for ourselves.

Does God rule your heart? Does He have your full attention? Make certain that the answer to both these questions is a resounding yes. In the life of every Christian, God should come first. And that's precisely the place that He deserves in your heart.

A Prayer to Start Your Day

Your faithfulness, Lord, is everlasting. Today let me serve You with my heart, my soul, and my mind. And then let me rest in the knowledge of Your unchanging and constant love for me. Amen.

25

Guard Your Thoughts

Finally brothers, whatever is true, whatever is honorable, whatever is just, whatever is pure, whatever is lovely, whatever is commendable–if there is any moral excellence and if there is any praise–dwell on these things.

PHILIPPIANS 4:8 HCSB

Because we are human, we are always busy with our thoughts. We simply can't help ourselves. Our brains never shut off, and even while we're sleeping, we mull things over in our minds. The question is not if we will think; the question is how we will think and what we will think about.

When we focus on the frustrations of today or the uncertainties of tomorrow, we rob ourselves of peace in the present moment. But when we direct our thoughts in more positive directions, we rob our worries of the power to tyrannize us.

The American poet Phoebe Cary observed, "All the great blessings of my life are present in my thoughts today." And her words apply to you. You will make your life better when you focus your thoughts on your blessings, not your misfortunes. So do yourself, your family, your friends, and your coworkers a favor: learn to think optimistically about the world you live in and the life you lead. Then prepare yourself for the blessings that good thoughts will bring.

A Prayer to Start Your Day

Dear Lord, when I am weak, I will turn to You for strength; when I am worried, I will turn to You for comfort; when I am troubled, I will turn to You for patience and perspective. Help me guard my thoughts, Lord, so that I may honor You this day and forever. Amen.

Be Patient and Trust God

Trust in Him at all times, you people;
pour out your heart before Him; God is a refuge for us.
PSALM 62:8 NKJV

Are you a person in a hurry? If so, you may be in for a few disappointments. Why? Because life has a way of unfolding according to its own timetable, not yours. That's why life requires patience, and lots of it.

Lamentations 3:25 reminds us that, "The LORD is good to those who wait for Him" (NKJV). But for most of us, waiting is difficult because we're in such a hurry for things to happen. We are fallible beings who seek solutions to our problems today, not tomorrow. Yet God may have other plans.

The next time you find your patience tested to the limit, slow down, take a deep breath, and relax. Sometimes life can't be hurried; during those times, patience is indeed a priceless virtue.

Patience is the companion of wisdom.
ST. AUGUSTINE

A Prayer to Start Your Day

Lord, give me patience. When I am hurried, give me peace. When I am frustrated, give me perspective. When I am angry, let me turn my heart to You. Today let me become a more patient person, dear Lord, as I trust in You and in Your master plan for my life. Amen.

27

Pray about Your Decisions

*But seek first the kingdom of God and His righteousness,
and all these things shall be added to you.*
MATTHEW 6:33 NKJV

Each day you must make countless decisions. Many of those decisions are so tightly woven into the fabric of your life that you scarcely realize they are decisions at all. Other decisions are made purely out of habit. But occasionally you'll find yourself at one of life's inevitable crossroads, and when you do, it's time to slow down and have a heart-to-heart talk with the ultimate Counselor, your Father in heaven.

If you're about to make an important decision, gather as much information as you can, and talk to trusted friends and family members. But above all, talk to God. He has a plan for your life and a purpose for your journey. He knows the next step you should take, so pray for guidance and listen carefully. He will never lead you astray.

The discipline of daily devotion to God undergirds decisions.
EDWIN LOUIS COLE

A Prayer to Start Your Day

Lord, help me to make decisions that are pleasing to You. Help me to be honest, patient, thoughtful, and obedient. And above all, help me to follow the teachings of Jesus, not just today but every day. Amen.

28

Know When to Say No

*So let us run the race that is before us and never give up.
We should remove from our lives anything that would
get in the way and the sin that so easily holds us back.*

HEBREWS 12:1 NCV

If you haven't yet learned to say no—to say it politely, firmly, and often—you're inviting untold stress into your life. Why? Because if you can't say no (when appropriate) to family members, friends, or coworkers, you'll find yourself overcommitted and underappreciated.

If you have trouble standing up for yourself, perhaps you're afraid that you'll be rejected. If so, here's a tip: Don't worry too much about rejection, especially when you're rejected for doing the right thing. You must never allow your "willingness to please" to interfere with your own good judgment or with God's priorities.

God gave you a conscience for a reason: to inform you about the things you need to do as well as the things you don't need to do. It's up to you to follow your conscience wherever it may lead, even if it means saying no.

*There are many burned-out people who think more is always better,
who deem it unspiritual to say no.*

SARAH YOUNG

A Prayer to Start Your Day

Dear Lord, when I need to say no, give me the courage, the wisdom, and the strength to say it. Today and every day, help me follow my conscience, not the crowd. Amen.

29

Share Your Christianity

Therefore, everyone who will acknowledge Me before men,
I will also acknowledge him before My Father in heaven.
MATTHEW 10:32 HCSB

Genuine, heartfelt Christianity can be highly contagious. When you've experienced the transforming power of God's love, you feel the need to share the Good News of His only begotten Son. So, whether you realize it or not, you can be sure that you are being led to share the story of your faith with family, with friends, and with the world.

Every believer, including you, bears responsibility for sharing God's Good News. And it is important to remember that you share your testimony through words and actions, but not necessarily in that order.

Today don't be bashful or timid. Talk about Jesus and, while you're at it, show the world what it really means to follow Him. After all, the fields are ripe for the harvest, time is short, and the workers are surprisingly few. So please share your story today because tomorrow may indeed be too late.

A Christian's purpose is to reach people with the gospel of Jesus Christ.
EDWIN LOUIS COLE

A Prayer to Start Your Day

Dear Lord, let me pause and reflect upon Christ's love, and let me share that love with all those who cross my path. And, as an expression of my love for Him, let me share Christ's transforming message with a world that desperately needs His grace. Amen.

30

Have the Courage to Trust God

Trust in the LORD with all your heart, and do not rely
on your own understanding; think about Him in all your ways,
and He will guide you on the right paths.

PROVERBS 3:5–6 HCSB

When our dreams come true and our plans prove successful, we find it easy to thank our Creator and easy to trust His divine providence. But in times of sorrow or hardship, we may find ourselves questioning God's plans for our lives.

On occasion, you will confront circumstances that trouble you to the very core of your soul. It is during these difficult days that you must find the wisdom and the courage to trust your heavenly Father despite your circumstances.

Are you a person who seeks God's blessings for yourself and your family? Then trust Him. Trust Him with your relationships. Trust Him with your priorities. Follow His commandments and pray for His guidance. Then wait patiently for God's revelations, and prepare yourself for the abundance and peace that will most certainly be yours when you do.

What you trust to Him you must not worry over
nor feel anxious about. Trust and worry cannot go together.

HANNAH WHITALL SMITH

A Prayer to Start Your Day

Dear Lord, let my faith be in You, and in You alone. Without You, I am weak, but when I trust You, I am protected. In every aspect of my life, Father, let me place my hope and my trust in Your infinite wisdom and Your boundless grace. Amen.

Make the Choice to Be Generous

The theme of generosity is woven into the fabric of God's Word. Our Creator instructs us to give generously—and cheerfully—to those in need. And He promises that when we do give of our time, our talents, and our resources, we will be blessed.

Jesus was the perfect example of generosity. He gave us everything, even His earthly life. He was always generous, always kind, always willing to help "the least of these." And if we are to follow in His footsteps, we, too, must be generous.

When you encounter a person in need, think of yourself as Christ's ambassador. And remember that whatever you do for the least of these, you also do for Him.

A Prayer to Start Your Day

Dear Lord, Your Word tells me that it is more blessed to give than to receive. Make me a faithful steward of the gifts You have given me, and let me share those gifts generously with others, today and every day that I live. Amen.

Pray without Ceasing

Prayer is a powerful tool that you can use to change your world and change yourself. God hears every prayer and responds in His own way and according to His own timetable. When you make a habit of consulting Him about everything, He'll guide you along a path of His choosing, which, by the way, is the path you should take. And when you petition Him for strength, He'll give you the courage to face any problem and the power to meet any challenge.

Today, instead of turning things over in your mind, turn them over to God in prayer. Take your concerns to the Lord and leave them there. Your heavenly Father is listening, and He wants to hear from you. Now.

A Prayer to Start Your Day

Dear Lord, Your holy Word commands me to pray without ceasing. In all things great and small, at all times, whether happy or sad, let me seek Your wisdom and Your strength . . . in prayer. Amen.

33

Keep Praying for Miracles

If you haven't seen any of God's miracles lately, you haven't been looking. Throughout history the Creator has intervened in the course of human events in ways that cannot be explained by science or human rationale. And He's still doing so today.

God's miracles are not limited to special occasions, nor are they witnessed by a select few. God is crafting His wonders all around us: the miracle of the birth of a new baby; the miracle of a world renewing itself with every sunrise; the miracle of lives transformed by God's love and grace. Each day, God's handiwork is evident for all to see and experience.

Today seize the opportunity to inspect God's handiwork. His miracles come in a variety of shapes and sizes, so keep your eyes and your heart open; you'll soon be amazed.

A Prayer to Start Your Day

Dear God, nothing is impossible for You. When I lose hope, give me faith; when others lose hope, let me tell them of Your glory and Your works. Today, Lord, let me expect the miraculous, and let me trust in You. Amen.

He Has Big Plans for You

Teach me to do Your will, for You are my God.
May Your gracious Spirit lead me on level ground.
PSALM 143:10 HCSB

God has a plan for this world and for your world. It's a plan that He understands perfectly, a plan that can bring you untold joy now and throughout eternity. But the Lord won't force His plan upon you. He's given you free will, the ability to make choices on your own. The totality of those choices will determine how well you fulfill God's calling.

Sometimes God makes Himself known in obvious ways, but more often His guidance is subtle. So we must be quiet to hear His voice.

If you're serious about discovering God's plan for your life—or rediscovering it—start spending quiet time with Him every day. Ask Him for direction. Pray for clarity. And be watchful for His signs. The more time you spend with Him, the sooner the answers will come.

You aren't an accident. You were deliberately planned, specifically gifted, and lovingly positioned on this earth by the Master Craftsman.
MAX LUCADO

A Prayer to Start Your Day

Dear Lord, I am Your creation, and You created me for a reason. Give me the wisdom to follow Your direction for my life's journey. Let me do Your work here on earth by seeking Your will and living it, knowing that when I trust in You, Father, I am eternally blessed. Amen.

35

He Is in Control

*Can you search out the deep things of God? Can you find out the
limits of the Almighty? They are higher than heaven—what can you do?
Deeper than Sheol—what can you know? Their measure
is longer than the earth and broader than the sea.*

JOB 11:7-9 NKJV

God is sovereign. He reigns over the entire universe and He
reigns over your little corner of that universe. Your challenge
is to recognize God's sovereignty, to live in accordance with
His commandments, and to trust His promises. Sometimes,
of course, these tasks are easier said than done.

Your heavenly Father may not always reveal Himself as
quickly (or as clearly) as you would like. But rest assured: God
is in control, God is here, and God intends to use you in wonderful, unexpected ways. He desires to lead you along a path
of His choosing. Your challenge is to watch, to listen, to learn
. . . and to follow. Today.

*One of the marks of spiritual maturity is the quiet confidence that God
is in control, without the need to understand why He does what He does.*

CHARLES SWINDOLL

A Prayer to Start Your Day

Dear Lord, You are the sovereign God of the universe. You rule
over our world, and I will allow You to rule over my heart. I
will seek Your will for my life, and I will allow Your Son to
reign over my heart today and every day of my life. Amen.

Seek Fellowship

Fellowship with other believers should be an integral part of your everyday life. Your association with fellow Christians will be uplifting, enlightening, encouraging *if* you find a group of friends who encourage you to pray more and worry less.

Are you an active member of your fellowship? Are you a builder of bridges inside the four walls of your church and outside it? Do you contribute to God's glory by contributing your time and your talents to a close-knit band of believers? I hope so. The fellowship of believers is intended to be a powerful tool for spreading God's Good News and uplifting His children. And God intends for you to be a fully contributing member of that fellowship. Your intentions should be the same.

A Prayer to Start Your Day

Heavenly Father, You have given me a community of supporters called the church. Let our fellowship be a reflection of the love we feel for each other and the love we feel for You. Amen.

Avoid the Distractions

All of us must live through those days when the traffic jams, the computer crashes, and the dog makes a main course out of our homework. But when we find ourselves distracted by the minor frustrations of life, we must catch ourselves, take a deep breath, and lift our thoughts upward.

Although we may, at times, struggle mightily to rise

above the distractions of everyday living, we need never struggle alone. God is here, eternal and faithful with infinite patience and love, and if we reach out to Him, He will restore our sense of perspective and give peace to our souls.

A Prayer to Start Your Day

Dear Lord, give me the wisdom to focus, not on the distractions of the moment, but on the priorities that matter. Today and every day, Father, guide my thoughts and guard my heart. Amen.

38

Do It Now

The old saying is both familiar and true: actions speak louder than words. And as believers, we must beware. Our actions should always give credence to the changes that Christ can make in the lives of those who walk with Him.

God calls upon each of us to act in accordance with His will and with respect for His commandments. If we are to be responsible believers, we must realize that it is never enough simply to hear the instructions of God; we must also live by them. And it is never enough to wait idly by while others do God's work here on earth; we, too, must act. Doing God's work is a responsibility that each of us must bear, and when we do, our loving heavenly Father rewards our efforts with a bountiful harvest.

A Prayer to Start Your Day

Dear Lord, let my words and deeds serve as a testimony to the changes You have made in my life. Let me praise You, Father, by following in the footsteps of Your Son, and let others see Him through me. Amen.

39

Be Determined to Serve

*Be strong and of good courage, and do it; do not fear
nor be dismayed, for the LORD God–my God–will be with you.
He will not leave you nor forsake you, until you have finished
all the work for the service of the house of the LORD.*

1 CHRONICLES 28:20 NKJV

Jesus teaches that the most esteemed men and women are not the self-congratulatory leaders of society but are instead the humblest of servants. But as weak human beings, we sometimes fall short as we seek to puff ourselves up and glorify our own accomplishments. To do so is wrong.

Today you may feel the temptation to build yourself up in the eyes of your neighbors. Resist that temptation. Instead, serve your neighbors quietly and without fanfare.

As a humble servant, you will glorify yourself, not before mankind, but before God, and that's what He intends. Earthly glory is fleeting but heavenly glory endures throughout eternity. So the choice is yours: either you can lift yourself up here on earth and be humbled in heaven, or vice versa.

Through our service to others, God wants to influence our world for Him.

VONETTE BRIGHT

A Prayer to Start Your Day

Dear Lord, in weak moments, we may try to build ourselves up by placing ourselves ahead of others. But You want us to be humble servants to those who need our encouragement, our help, and our love. Today we will do our best to follow in the footsteps of Your Son Jesus by serving others humbly, faithfully, and lovingly. Amen.

40

Distrust the Media's Distorted Messages

Do not love the world or the things that belong to the world.
If anyone loves the world, love for the Father is not in him.

1 JOHN 2:15 HCSB

Sometimes it's hard to stand firm in your faith, especially when the world keeps pumping out messages that are contrary to your beliefs.

The media is working around the clock in an attempt to rearrange your priorities. The media says that appearance is all-important, that social standing is all-important. These messages are untrue. The important things in life have little to do with appearances. The all-important things in life have to do with your faith, your family, and your future. Period.

Living in the twenty-first century, you are relentlessly bombarded by media messages that are contrary to your faith. Take those messages with a grain of salt—or not at all.

Our fight is not against any physical enemy; it is against organizations and powers that are spiritual. We must struggle against sin all our lives, but we are assured we will win.

CORRIE TEN BOOM

A Prayer to Start Your Day

Lord, this world is filled with temptations and distractions; we have many opportunities to stray from Your commandments. Help us to focus, not on the things of this world, but on the message of Your Son. Let us keep Christ in our hearts as we follow Him this day and forever. Amen.

Keep Recharging Your Batteries

*Dear brothers and sisters, I close my letter with these last words:
Be joyful. Grow to maturity. Encourage each other. Live in harmony
and peace. Then the God of love and peace will be with you.*

2 CORINTHIANS 13:11 NLT

Even the most faithful believers can, from time to time, find themselves running on empty. The demands of daily life can drain us of our strength and rob us of the joy that is rightfully ours in Christ. When we find ourselves tired, discouraged, anxious, or worse, there is a source from which we can draw the power needed to recharge our spiritual batteries. That source is God.

Are you tired or troubled? Turn your heart toward God in prayer. Are you weak or worried? Take the time—or, more accurately, make the time—to delve deeply into God's holy Word. Are you spiritually depleted? Call upon fellow believers to support you, and call upon Christ to renew your spirit and your life. When you do, you'll discover that the Creator of the universe stands always ready and always able to create a new sense of wonderment and joy in you.

*One of the greatest techniques of human well-being
is surrendering yourself to the recuperative power of God.*

NORMAN VINCENT PEALE

A Prayer to Start Your Day

Dear Lord, sometimes I grow weary; sometimes I am discouraged; sometimes I am fearful. Yet when I turn my heart and my prayers to You, I am secure. Renew my strength, Father, and let me draw comfort and courage from Your promises and from Your unending love. Amen.

Be a Faithful Steward
of God's Gifts

*God has given each of you a gift from his great variety
of spiritual gifts. Use them well to serve one another.*

1 PETER 4:10 NLT

The gifts that you possess are blessings from the Giver of all
things good. Do you have a spiritual gift? Share it. Do you
have a testimony about the things that Christ has done for
you? Don't leave your story untold. Do you possess financial
resources? Share them. Do you have particular talents? Hone
your skills and use them for God's glory.

All your talents, all your opportunities, and all your gifts
are on temporary loan from the Creator. Use those gifts while
you can because time is short and the needs are great. In every
undertaking, make God your partner. Then, just as He promised, God will bless you now and forever.

Today and every day, be a faithful steward of your talents
and your treasures. And then prepare yourself for even greater
blessings that are sure to come.

*If others don't use their gifts, you get cheated,
and if you don't use your gifts, they get cheated.*

RICK WARREN

A Prayer to Start Your Day

Dear Lord, let me use my gifts, and let me help others discover theirs. Your gifts are priceless and eternal. May we, Your
children, use them to the glory of Your kingdom, today and
forever. Amen.

43

Make Peace with Your Past

Do not remember the past events, pay no attention to things of old. Look, I am about to do something new; even now it is coming. Do you not see it? Indeed, I will make a way in the wilderness, rivers in the desert.

ISAIAH 43:18–19 HCSB

Since we can't change the pains and disappointments of the past, why do so many of us insist upon replaying them over and over again in our minds? Perhaps it's because we can't find it in our hearts to forgive the people who have hurt us. Being mere mortals, we seek revenge, not reconciliation, and we harbor hatred in our hearts, sometimes for decades.

Obviously, we cannot change the past. It is what it was and forever will be. The present, of course, is a different matter.

Today is filled with opportunities to live, to love, to work, to play, and to celebrate life. If we sincerely wish to build a better tomorrow, we can start building it today, in the present moment. So if you've endured a difficult past, accept it, learn from it, and forgive everybody, including yourself. Once you've made peace with your past, don't spend too much time there. Instead, live in the precious present, where opportunities abound and change is still possible.

The past cannot be changed, but one's response to it can be.

ERWIN LUTZER

A Prayer to Start Your Day

Heavenly Father, free me from anger, resentment, and envy. When I am bitter, I cannot feel the peace that You intend for my life. Help me accept the past, treasure the present, and trust the future to You. Amen.

44

Dream Big Dreams

With God's power working in us, God can do much,
much more than anything we can ask or imagine.
EPHESIANS 3:20 NCV

Are you willing to entertain the possibility that God has big plans in store for you? I hope so. Yet sometimes, especially if you've recently experienced a life-altering disappointment, you may find it difficult to envision a brighter future for yourself and your family. If so, it's time to reconsider your own capabilities . . . and God's.

Your heavenly Father created you with unique gifts and untapped talents. When you tap into them, you'll begin to feel an increasing sense of confidence in yourself and in your future.

It takes courage to dream big dreams. You will discover that courage when you do three things: accept the past, trust God to handle the future, and make the most of the time He has given you today.

Nothing is too difficult for God, and no dreams are too big for Him—not even yours. So start living—and dreaming—accordingly.

Allow your dreams a place in your prayers and plans. God-given
dreams can help you move into the future He is preparing for you.
BARBARA JOHNSON

A Prayer to Start Your Day

Dear Lord, give me the courage to dream and to trust in Your perfect plan. When I am worried or weary, give me strength for today and hope for tomorrow. Keep me mindful of Your healing power, infinite love, and eternal salvation. Amen.

45

Be a Source of Encouragement

May the patience and encouragement that come from God allow you to live in harmony with each other the way Christ Jesus wants.
ROMANS 15:5 NCV

Are you a continuing source of encouragement to your family and friends? One of the reasons that God put you here is to serve and encourage other people, starting with the people who live under your roof.

As a follower of the One from Galilee, you have the opportunity to become a beacon of encouragement to the world. How can you do it? By looking for the good in others and celebrating the good that you find. As the old saying goes, "When someone does something good, applaud. You'll make two people happy!"

Even a brief word of appreciation can make a big difference in someone's life. So how many people will you encourage today? Ten? Twenty? Even more than that? The answer you give will help determine the quality of their lives *and* the quality of yours.

Kind words can be short and easy to speak,
but their echoes are truly endless.
MOTHER TERESA

A Prayer to Start Your Day

Dear Lord, let me celebrate the accomplishments of others. Make me a source of genuine, lasting encouragement to my family and friends. And let my words and deeds be worthy of Your Son, the One who gives me strength and salvation, this day and for all eternity. Amen.

Pray about Your Decisions

Now if any of you lacks wisdom, he should ask God, who gives to all generously and without criticizing, and it will be given to him. But let him ask in faith without doubting. For the doubter is like the surging sea, driven and tossed by the wind.
JAMES 1:5–6 HCSB

Have you asked God for His guidance in every aspect of your life? If so, then you're continually inviting your Creator to reveal Himself in a variety of ways. As a follower of Christ, you must do no less.

Jesus made it clear to His disciples: they should pray always. So should we. Heartfelt prayer produces powerful changes in us and in our world. When we lift our hearts to our Father in heaven, we open ourselves to a never-ending source of divine wisdom.

Do you have questions about your future that you simply can't answer? Ask for the guidance of your heavenly Father. Do you sincerely seek to know God's purpose for your life? Then ask Him for direction—and keep asking Him every day that you live. Whatever your need, no matter how great or small, pray about it and never lose hope. God is not just near; He is here, and He's ready to talk with you right now.

When there is a matter that requires definite prayer, pray until you believe God and until you can thank Him for His answer.
HANNAH WHITALL SMITH

A Prayer to Start Your Day

Dear Lord, today and every day I will pray about matters great and small. I bring my concerns to You, Father. I will listen for Your voice, and I will follow in the footsteps of Your Son. Amen.

47

Cease Complaining

Most of us have more blessings than we can count, yet we can still find reasons to complain about the minor frustrations of everyday life. To do so, of course, is not only shortsighted, but it is also a serious roadblock on the path to spiritual abundance.

Would you like to feel more comfortable about your circumstances and your life? Then promise yourself that you'll do whatever it takes to ensure that you focus your thoughts and energy on the major blessings you've received, not the minor inconveniences you must occasionally endure.

So the next time you're tempted to complain about the inevitable frustrations of everyday living, don't do it. Make it a practice to count your blessings, not your hardships.

A Prayer to Start Your Day

Lord, I know that the choice is mine—I can either count my blessings or complain about my disappointments. Today help me to focus my thoughts upon my blessings, my gifts, and my opportunities. Amen.

48

Let God Be the Judge

The Bible instructs us to avoid the temptation to judge others. Yet even the most thoughtful among us may fall prey to a powerful yet subtle temptation: the temptation to judge.

As Jesus came upon a young woman who had been condemned by the Pharisees, He spoke not only to the crowd that was gathered there but also to all generations when He warned, "He that is without sin among you, let him first cast a stone at her" (John 8:7 KJV). Christ's message is clear, and it applies not only to the Pharisees of ancient times, but also to us.

So the next time you're beset by the temptation to judge another human being's motives, catch yourself before you make that mistake. Don't be a judge; be a witness.

A Prayer to Start Your Day

Dear Lord, You have commanded me not to judge. Keep me mindful, Father, that when I judge others, I am living outside of Your will for my life. You have forgiven me, Lord. Let me forgive others, let me love them, and let me help them . . . without judging them. Amen.

49

Ask Him for the Things You Need

God invites us to ask Him for the things we need, and He promises to hear our prayers as well as our thoughts. The Lord is always available, and He's always ready to help us. And He knows precisely what we need. But He still instructs us to ask.

Do you make a habit of asking God for the things you need? I hope so. After all, the Father has a plan for your life. And He can do great things through you if you have the courage to ask for His guidance and His help. So don't hesitate to ask Him for the tools needed to accomplish His plan for your life. Then get busy and expect the best. When you do your part, God will certainly do His part. Great things are bound to happen.

A Prayer to Start Your Day

Dear Lord, today I will ask You for the things I need. In every circumstance, in every season of life, I will come to You in prayer. You know the desires of my heart, Lord; grant them, I ask. Yet not my will, Father, but Your will be done. Amen.

50

Forgive Difficult People

But the wisdom that comes from God is first of all pure, then peaceful, gentle, and easy to please. This wisdom is always ready to help those who are troubled and to do good for others. It is always fair and honest.

JAMES 3:17 NCV

Sometimes people can be discourteous and cruel. Sometimes people can be unfair, unkind, and unappreciative. Sometimes people get angry and frustrated. So what's a Christian to do? God's answer is straightforward: forgive, forget, and move on. In Luke 6:37, Jesus instructs, "Do not judge, and you will not be judged. Do not condemn, and you will not be condemned. Forgive, and you will be forgiven" (HCSB). So be quick to forgive others for their shortcomings. And when other people misbehave (as they most certainly will from time to time), don't pay too much attention. Just forgive those people and move on as quickly as you can.

We must meet our disappointments, our malicious enemies, our provoking friends, our trials of every sort, with an attitude of surrender and trust. We must rise above them in Christ so they lose their power to harm us.

HANNAH WHITALL SMITH

A Prayer to Start Your Day

Dear Lord, when people around me are difficult, give me perspective and faith. When I am weak, give me strength to forgive. Let me trust in Your promises, Father, and let me live with the assurance that You are with me not only today but also throughout all eternity. Amen.

Beware of Your Adversary

So humble yourselves before God.
Resist the devil, and he will flee from you.
JAMES 4:7 NLT

This world is God's creation, and it contains the wonderful fruits of His handiwork. But, the world also contains countless opportunities to stray from God's will. Temptations are everywhere, and the devil never takes a day off. Our task as believers is to turn away from temptation and to place our lives squarely in the center of God's will.

In his letter to Jewish Christians, Peter offered a stern warning: "Your adversary, the devil, prowls around like a roaring lion, seeking someone to devour" (1 Peter 5:8 NASB). What was true in New Testament times is equally true in our own. Evil is indeed abroad in the world, and Satan continues to sow the seeds of destruction far and wide. As Christians, we must guard our hearts by earnestly wrapping ourselves in the protection of God's holy Word. When we do, we are protected.

Measure your growth in grace by your sensitivity to sin.
OSWALD CHAMBERS

A Prayer to Start Your Day

Dear Lord, because You have given Your children free will, the world is a place where evil threatens our lives and our souls. Protect us, Father, from the evils and temptations of this difficult age. Help us to trust You, Father, and to obey Your Word, knowing that Your ultimate victory over evil is both inevitable and complete. Amen.

52

Say No to Envy

God's Word warns us about a dangerous, destructive state of mind: envy. Envy is emotional poison. It poisons the mind and hardens the heart.

If we are to experience the abundant lives that Christ has promised, we must be on guard against envious thoughts. Jealousy breeds discontent, discontent breeds unhappiness, and unhappiness robs us of the peace that might otherwise be ours.

So if the sin of envy has invaded your heart, ask God to help you heal. When you ask sincerely, and when He responds, you'll regain the peace that can only be found through Him.

A Prayer to Start Your Day
Dear Lord, deliver me from the needless pain of envy. You have given me countless blessings. Let me be thankful for the gifts I have received, and let me never be resentful of the gifts You have given others. Amen.

53

Say No to Anger

Sometimes anger is appropriate. Even Jesus became angry when confronted with the moneychangers in the temple. On occasion you, like Jesus, will confront evil, and when you do, you may respond as He did: vigorously and without reservation. But more often than not, your frustrations will be of the more mundane variety.

As long as you live here on earth, you will face countless opportunities to lose your temper over small, relatively insignificant events: a traffic jam, a spilled cup of coffee, an inconsiderate comment, a broken promise. When you are tempted to lose your temper over the minor inconveniences of life, don't. Turn away from anger, hatred, bitterness, and regret. Turn instead to God.

A Prayer to Start Your Day

Dear Lord, help me to turn away from angry thoughts. Help me always to use Jesus as my guide for life, and let me trust His promises today and forever. Amen.

54

Celebrate Life Every Day

Psalm 100 reminds us that we should "shout to the Lord, all the earth. Serve the LORD with joy; come before him with singing" (vv. 1–2 NCV). As God's children, we are blessed beyond measure, but sometimes, as busy people living in a demanding world, we are slow to count our gifts and even slower to give thanks to the Giver.

Our blessings include life and health, family and friends, freedom and possessions—for starters. And the gifts we receive from God are multiplied when we share them.

The 118th Psalm reminds us that each day is a gift from the Creator, and it's our responsibility to celebrate both the gift and the Giver. So with no further ado, let the celebration begin!

A Prayer to Start Your Day

Dear Lord, help us remember that every day is cause for celebration. Today we will try our best to keep joy in our hearts. We will celebrate the life You have given us here on earth and the eternal life that will be ours in heaven. Amen.

Keep It Simple

*But godliness with contentment is a great gain. For we brought
nothing into the world, and we can take nothing out. But if we have
food and clothing, we will be content with these. But those who want
to be rich fall into temptation, a trap, and many foolish and harmful
desires, which plunge people into ruin and destruction.*

1 TIMOTHY 6:6–9 HCSB

You live in a world where simplicity is in short supply. Think
for a moment about the complexity of your everyday life and
compare it to the lives of your ancestors. Certainly, you are
the beneficiary of many technological innovations, but those
innovations have a price: in all likelihood, your world is highly
complex. Consequently, you have too many distractions (if
you choose to let them distract you) and too many things to
worry about (if you choose to worry about them).

Unless you take firm control of your time and your life,
you may be overwhelmed by an ever-increasing tidal wave of
complexity that threatens your happiness and your sanity. But
your heavenly Father understands the joy of living simply. So
do yourself a favor: keep your life as simple as possible. By
simplifying your life, you are destined to improve it.

*Out of the freedom from worry that God's generosity provides comes
an impulse toward simplicity rather than accumulation.*

JOHN PIPER

A Prayer to Start Your Day

Dear Lord, help me understand the joys of simplicity. Life
is complicated enough without my adding to the confusion.
Wherever I happen to be, help me to keep it simple—very
simple. Amen.

Make the Most of Whatever Comes

People may make plans in their minds,
but the LORD decides what they will do.
PROVERBS 16:9 NCV

Sometimes we must accept life on its terms, not our own. Life has a way of unfolding, not as we will, but as it will. And sometimes there is precious little we can do to change things.

When events transpire that are beyond our control, we have a choice: we can either learn the art of acceptance, or we can make ourselves miserable as we struggle to change the unchangeable.

We must entrust the things we cannot change to God. When we do, we can prayerfully and faithfully tackle the important work that He has placed before us: doing something about the things we can change, and doing it sooner rather than later.

Can you summon the courage and the wisdom to accept life on its own terms? If so, you'll most certainly be rewarded for your good judgment.

Accept each day as it comes to you. Do not waste your time
and energy wishing for a different set of circumstances.
SARAH YOUNG

A Prayer to Start Your Day

Dear Lord, let me live in the present, not the past. Give me the wisdom to be thankful for the gifts that I do have, and not bitter about the things that I don't have. Let me accept what was; let me give thanks for what is; and, let me have faith in what most surely will be: the promise of eternal life with You. Amen.

Answer the Call

I urge you who have been chosen by God
to live up to the life to which God called you.
EPHESIANS 4:1 NCV

Whether you realize it or not, God is calling you to follow a specific path that He has chosen for your life. And it is vitally important that you heed that call. Otherwise, your talents and opportunities may go unused.

Have you already heard God's call? And are you pursuing it with vigor? If so, you're both fortunate and wise. But if you have not yet discovered what God intends for you to do with your life, keep searching and keep praying until you discover why the Creator put you here.

God has important work for you to do—work that no one else on earth can accomplish but you. The Creator has placed you in a particular location, amid particular people, with unique opportunities to serve. And He has given you all the tools you need to succeed. So listen for His voice, watch for His signs, and prepare yourself for the call that is sure to come.

God's call is an inner conviction given by the Holy Spirit
and confirmed by the Word of God and the body of Christ.
ERWIN LUTZER

A Prayer to Start Your Day

Heavenly Father, You have called me, and I acknowledge that calling. In these quiet moments before this busy day unfolds, I will seek Your guidance. Give me the wisdom to know Your will for my life and the courage to follow wherever You may lead me, today and forever. Amen.

Find Contentment in All the Right Places

I am the door. If anyone enters by Me, he will be saved and will come in and go out and find pasture.
JOHN 10:9 HCSB

Where can you find contentment? Is it a result of wealth or power or beauty or fame? Hardly. Genuine contentment springs from a peaceful spirit, a clear conscience, and a loving heart (like yours!).

Our modern world seems preoccupied with the search for happiness. We are bombarded with messages telling us that happiness depends upon aquiring material possessions. These messages are false. Peace is not the result of our acquisitions; it is the result of our dispositions. If we don't find contentment within ourselves, we will never find it outside ourselves.

Thus the search for contentment is an internal quest, an exploration of the heart, mind, and soul. You can find contentment—indeed you will find it—if you simply look in the right places. And the best time to start looking in those places is now.

Contentment is possible when we stop striving for more.
CHARLES SWINDOLL

A Prayer to Start Your Day

Father, let me be a faithful servant who strives to do Your will, and as I do, let me find contentment and balance. Let me live in the light of Your will and Your priorities for my life, and when I have done my best, Lord, give me the wisdom to place my faith and my trust in You. Amen.

59

Guard Your Heart and Mind

God's Word is clear: we are to guard our hearts "above all else," yet we live in world that encourages us to do otherwise. Here in the twenty-first century, temptations and distractions are woven into the fabric of everyday life. As believers, we must remain vigilant. We must resist the devil when he confronts us, and avoid those places where Satan can most easily tempt us.

Every day, you are faced with more choices than you can count. You can do the right thing, or not. You can be kind, and generous, and obedient to God. Or not. Today, the world offers countless opportunities to let down your guard and thereby we make needless mistakes that may injure you or your loved ones. So guard your heart by giving it to your heavenly Father; it is safe with Him.

A Prayer to Start Your Day

Dear Lord, I will guard my heart against the evils, the temptations, and the distractions of this world. I will focus, instead, upon Your love, Your blessings, and Your Son. Amen.

60

Follow Him

Jesus walks with you. Are you walking with Him? I hope you will choose to walk with Him today and every day of your life.

Jesus loved you so much that He endured unspeakable humiliation and suffering for you. How will you respond to Christ's sacrifice? Will you take up your cross and follow Him (Luke 9:23) or will you choose another path? When you place your hopes squarely at the foot of the cross, and place Jesus squarely at the center of your life, you will be blessed. If you seek to be a worthy disciple of Jesus, you must acknowledge that He is always first. So pick up your cross today and every day that you live. You will quickly discover that Christ's love has the power to change everything, including you.

A Prayer to Start Your Day

Dear Jesus, because I am Your disciple, I will trust You, I will obey Your teachings, and I will share Your Good News. You have given me life abundant and life eternal, and I will follow You today and forever. Amen.

61

Be a Cheerful Christian

On some days it's hard to be cheerful. Sometimes, as the demands of the world increase and our energy sags, we feel less like "cheering up" and more like "tearing up." But even in our darkest hours, we can turn to God, and He will give us comfort.

Few things in life are more sad than a grumpy Christian. Christ promises us lives of abundance and joy, but He does not force His joy upon us. We must claim His joy for ourselves, and when we do, Jesus fills our spirits with His power and His love.

How can we receive from Christ the joy that is rightfully ours? By giving Him what is rightfully His: our hearts and our souls. Then we can share His joy and His message with a world that needs both.

A Prayer to Start Your Day

Dear Lord, help me choose an attitude of cheerfulness. Let me be a joyful Christian, quick to smile and slow to anger. And let me share Your goodness with all whom I meet so that Your love might shine in me and through me. Amen.

Discover the Power of Silence

Truly my soul silently waits for God; from Him comes my salvation.
PSALM 62:1 NKJV

The world seems to grow louder day by day, and our senses seem to be invaded at every turn. If we allow the distractions of a clamorous society to separate us from God's peace, we do ourselves a profound disservice. Instead, we should carve out moments of silence amid the sea of noise.

If we are to maintain righteous minds and compassionate hearts, we must take time each day for prayer and for meditation. We must make ourselves still in the presence of our Creator. We must quiet our minds and our hearts so that we might sense God's will and His love.

So even if your appointment book is filled from cover to cover, make time for silence. You should always have at least one serious chat with your Creator every day. He deserves it. And so, by the way, do you.

Nothing can calm our souls more, or better prepare us for life's challenges, than time spent alone with God.
BILLY GRAHAM

A Prayer to Start Your Day

Dear Lord, help me remember the importance of silence. Help me discover quiet moments throughout the day so that I can sense Your presence and Your love. Amen.

Abound in Love

And may the Lord make you increase
and abound in love to one another and to all.

1 THESSALONIANS 3:12 NKJV

Christ showed His love for us by willingly sacrificing His own life so that we might have eternal life: "But God demonstrates His own love toward us, in that while we were still sinners, Christ died for us" (Romans 5:8). We, as Christ's followers, are challenged to share His love with kind words on our lips and praise in our hearts.

Just as Christ has been—and will always be—the ultimate friend to His flock, so should we be Christ-like in the kindness and generosity that we show toward others, especially those who are most in need.

When we walk each day with Jesus—and obey the commandments found in God's holy Word—we become worthy ambassadors for Christ. When we share the love of Christ, we share a priceless gift with the world. As His servants, we must do no less.

Let no one ever come to you without leaving better and happier.
Be the living expression of God's kindness.

MOTHER TERESA

A Prayer to Start Your Day

Dear Lord, today let me share kind words in honor of Your Son. Today let forgiveness rule my heart. And every day, Lord, let my love for Christ be reflected through my actions as I serve those who need the loving touch of the Master's hand. Amen.

Be a Worthy Disciple

He has told you what is good and what it is the LORD requires of you:
to act justly, to love faithfulness, and to walk humbly with your God.
MICAH 6:8 HCSB

When Jesus addressed His disciples, He warned that each one must "take up his cross and follow Me." The disciples must have known exactly what the Master meant. In Jesus's day, prisoners were forced to carry their own crosses to the location where they would be put to death. Christ's message was clear: in order to follow Him, Christ's disciples must deny themselves and, instead, trust Him completely.

If we are to be disciples of Christ, we must trust Him and place Him at the very center of our beings. Jesus never comes "next." He is always first. The paradox, of course, is that only by sacrificing ourselves to Him do we gain salvation for ourselves.

Do you seek to be a worthy disciple of Christ? Then pick up your cross today and every day that you live. When you do, He will bless you now and forever.

A disciple is a follower of Christ. That means you
take on His priorities as your own. His agenda
becomes your agenda. His mission becomes your mission.
CHARLES STANLEY

A Prayer to Start Your Day

Dear Lord, thank You for the gift of Your Son. Let me be His worthy disciple. I offer my life to You, Lord, so that I might live according to Your commandments and according to Your plan. I will praise You always as I give thanks for Your Son and for Your everlasting love. Amen.

Defeat Procrastination

*When you make a vow to God, don't delay fulfilling it,
because He does not delight in fools. Fulfill what you vow.*
ECCLESIASTES 5:4 HCSB

There's never a "perfect" time to do anything. That's why we can always find reasons to put off until tomorrow the things that we should be doing today.

If you find yourself bound by the chains of procrastination, ask yourself what you're waiting for—or more accurately what you're afraid of—and why. As you examine the emotional roadblocks that have heretofore blocked your path, you may discover that you're waiting for the "perfect" moment, that instant in time when you feel neither afraid nor anxious. But in truth, perfect moments like these are few and far between.

So stop waiting for the perfect moment and focus, instead, on finding the right moment to do what needs to be done. Then trust God and get busy. When you do, you'll discover that you and the Father, working together, can accomplish great things . . . and that you can accomplish them sooner rather than later.

*If you are facing a difficult task don't put it off.
If you do it will just keep tormenting you.*
JOYCE MEYER

A Prayer to Start Your Day

Dear Lord, when I am confronted with things that need to be done, give me the courage and the wisdom to do them now, not later. Amen.

Pray for God's Abundance

*I have come that they may have life,
and that they may have it more abundantly.*
JOHN 10:10 NKJV

The familiar words of John 10:10 should serve as a daily reminder: Christ came to this earth so that we might experience His abundance, His love, and His gift of eternal life. But Christ does not force Himself upon us; we must claim His gifts for ourselves.

Of course, some days are so busy and so hurried that abundance seems a distant promise. It is not. Every day, we can claim the spiritual abundance that God promises for our lives, and we should.

Today will you claim the only kind of abundance that really matters? Will you slow yourself down long enough to ask your heavenly Father for guidance and protection? Will you claim His spiritual riches and experience His peace? You can, and you should. God's abundance is available to all. Accept it, and be blessed.

*Knowing that your future is absolutely assured
can free you to live abundantly today.*
SARAH YOUNG

A Prayer to Start Your Day

Dear Lord, thank You for the abundant life that can be mine through Christ Jesus. Guide me according to Your will, and help me be a worthy example to others. Give me courage, Lord, to claim the spiritual riches that You have promised, and show me Your plan for my life, today and forever. Amen.

Trust God's Wisdom

Insight is a fountain of life for its possessor,
but the discipline of fools is folly.
PROVERBS 16:22 HCSB

Where will you place your trust today? Will you trust in the wisdom of fallible men and women, or will you place your faith in God's perfect wisdom? When you decide whom to trust, you will then know how best to respond to the challenges of the coming day.

Are you tired? Discouraged? Fearful? Be comforted and trust God. Are you worried or anxious? Be confident in God's power and trust His holy Word. Are you confused? Listen to the quiet voice of your heavenly Father. He is not a God of confusion. Talk with Him; listen to Him; trust Him. He is steadfast, and He is your Protector, now and forever.

The more wisdom enters our hearts, the more we
will be able to trust our hearts in difficult situations.
JOHN ELDREDGE

A Prayer to Start Your Day

Dear Lord, You are my Teacher. Help me to learn from Your wisdom. And then, let me show others what it means to be a kind, generous, loving Christian. Amen.

68

Beware of Bitterness

Hatred stirs up conflicts, but love covers all offenses.
PROVERBS 10:12 HCSB

Are you mired in the quicksand of bitterness or regret? If so, it's time to free yourself from the mire. The world holds few if any rewards for those who remain angrily focused upon the past. Still, the act of forgiveness is difficult for all but the most saintly men and women.

Being frail, fallible, imperfect beings, most of us are quick to anger, quick to blame, slow to forgive, and even slower to forget. Yet we know that it's best to forgive others, just as we, too, have been forgiven.

If there exists even one person—including yourself—against whom you still harbor bitter feelings, it's time to forgive and move on. Bitterness and regret are not part of God's plan for you, but God won't force you to forgive others. It's a job that only you can finish, and the sooner you finish it, the better.

Bitterness imprisons life; love releases it.
HARRY EMERSON FOSDICK

A Prayer to Start Your Day

Heavenly Father, free me from anger and bitterness. Keep me mindful that forgiveness is Your commandment. Let me turn away from bitterness and instead claim the spiritual abundance that You offer through the gift of Your Son. Amen.

69

Consider the Possibilities

*But Jesus looked at them and said, "With men this is impossible,
but with God all things are possible."*
MATTHEW 19:26 HCSB

All of us must endure difficult days. Sometimes even the most optimistic Christians can become discouraged, and you are no exception. If you're being tested by trying circumstances, perhaps it's time to focus more on your strengths and less on the challenges that confront you.

Every day, including this one, is brimming with possibilities. Every day is filled with opportunities to grow, to serve, and to share. But if you're entangled in a web of worry, you may overlook the blessings that God has scattered along your path.

So don't give in to pessimism, to doubt, to negativity, or to cynicism. Instead, keep your eyes upon the possibilities, fix your heart upon the Creator, do your best, and let Him handle the rest.

Without faith, nothing is possible. With it, nothing is impossible.
MARY McLEOD BETHUNE

A Prayer to Start Your Day

Dear God, nothing is impossible for You. Your infinite power is beyond human understanding—keep me always mindful of Your strength. When I lose hope, give me faith; when others lose hope, let me tell them of Your glory and Your works. Today, Lord, let me expect the miraculous, and let me trust in You. Amen.

Consider This Day
a New Beginning

Then the One seated on the throne said,
"Look! I am making everything new."
REVELATION 21:5 HCSB

Each new day offers countless opportunities to serve God, to seek His will, and to obey His teachings. But each day also offers countless opportunities to stray from God's commandments and to wander far from His path.

Sometimes we wander aimlessly in a wilderness of our own making, but God has better plans for each of us. Consequently, whenever we ask Him to renew our strength and guide our steps, He does so.

Consider this day a new beginning. Consider it a fresh start, a renewed opportunity to serve your Creator with willing hands and a loving heart. Ask the Lord to renew your sense of purpose. Ask Him for courage and guidance. Ask for the wisdom to trust your hopes, not your fears. When you ask, you will receive because He always keeps His promises. Always.

The amazing thing about Jesus is that He doesn't just patch up our lives, He gives us a brand new sheet, a clean slate to start over, all new.
GLORIA GAITHER

A Prayer to Start Your Day

Dear Lord, You have the power to make all things new. Renew my strength, Father, and renew my hope for the future. Today and every day, Lord, let me draw comfort and courage from Your promises and from Your unending love. Amen.

Develop a Faith that Can Move Mountains

I assure you: If anyone says to this mountain, "Be lifted up and thrown into the sea," and does not doubt in his heart, but believes that what he says will happen, it will be done for him.

MARK 11:23 HCSB

When a suffering woman sought healing by simply touching the hem of His garment, Jesus turned and said, "Daughter, be of good comfort; thy faith hath made thee whole" (Matthew 9:22 KJV). We, too, can be made whole when we place our faith completely and unwaveringly in the person of Jesus Christ.

Concentration-camp survivor Corrie ten Boom relied on faith during her ten months of imprisonment and torture. Later, despite the fact that four of her family members had died in Nazi death camps, Corrie's faith was unshaken. She wrote, "There is no pit so deep that God's love is not deeper still." Christians take note: genuine faith in God means faith in all circumstances, happy or sad, joyful or tragic.

If your faith is being tested to the point of breaking, know that Your Savior is near. If you reach out to Him in faith, He will give you peace and heal your broken spirit. Be content to touch even the smallest fragment of the Master's garment, and He will make you whole.

A Prayer to Start Your Day

Dear Lord, help me to be a person of faith. Help me to remember that You are always near and that You can overcome any challenge. With Your love and Your power, Lord, I can live courageously and faithfully today and every day. Amen.

72
Get Involved in a Church

For where two or three are gathered together in My name,
I am there in the midst of them.
MATTHEW 18:20 NKJV

Are you an active, contributing member of your local fellowship? The answer to this simple question will have a profound impact on the direction of your spiritual journey.

Do yourself a favor: Find a congregation you're comfortable with and join it. After you've joined, don't just attend church out of habit. Go to church out of a sincere desire to know and worship God. When you do, you'll be blessed by the men and women who attend your fellowship, and you'll be blessed by your Creator.

A Prayer to Start Your Day

Dear Lord, today I pray for Your church. Help me to feed Your flock by helping to build Your church so that others, too, might experience Your enduring love and Your eternal grace. Amen.

73
Be Aware of Your Blessings

Psalm 145:8–9 makes this promise: "The LORD is gracious and compassionate, slow to anger and rich in love. The LORD is good to all; he has compassion on all he has made" (NIV). As God's children, we are blessed beyond measure, but sometimes we are slow to count our gifts and even slower to give thanks to the Giver.

Our blessings include life and health, family and friends, freedom and possessions. And the gifts we receive from God are multiplied when we share them with others. May we always give thanks to God for our blessings, and may we always demonstrate our gratitude by sharing them.

A Prayer to Start Your Day

Lord, let me count my blessings, and let me be Your faithful servant as I give praise to the Giver of all things good.

74

Let God Guide the Way

The true children of God are those who let God's Spirit lead them.
ROMANS 8:14 NCV

The Bible promises that God will guide you if you let Him. Your job, of course, is to let Him. But sometimes you will be tempted to do otherwise. Sometimes you'll be tempted to go along with the crowd; other times, you'll be tempted to do things your way, not God's way. When you feel those temptations, resist them.

What will you allow to guide you through the coming day: your own desires (or, for that matter, the desires of your friends)? Or will you allow God to lead the way? The answer should be obvious. You should let God be your guide. When you entrust your life to Him completely and without reservation, God will give you the strength to meet any challenge, the courage to face any trial, and the wisdom to live in His righteousness. So trust Him today and seek His guidance. When you do, your next step will be the right one.

A Prayer to Start Your Day

Lord, You have a plan for my life. Let me discover it and live it. Today I will seek Your will, knowing that when I trust in You, dear Father, I am eternally blessed. Amen.

Give Your Anxiety to God

Anxiety in a man's heart weighs it down, but a good word cheers it up.
PROVERBS 12:25 HCSB

When calamity strikes anywhere in the world, we may be confronted with real-time images, images that breed anxiety. And as we stare transfixed at our television screens, we may fall prey to fear, discouragement, worry, or all three. But our Father in heaven has other plans. God has promised that we may lead lives of abundance, not anxiety. In fact, His Word instructs us to "be anxious for nothing" (Philippians 4:6 NASB). But how can we put our fears to rest? By taking those fears to God and leaving them there.

As you face the challenges of daily life, you may find yourself becoming anxious. If so, turn every one of your concerns over to your heavenly Father. The same God who created the universe will comfort you if you ask Him, so ask Him and trust Him. And then watch in amazement as your anxieties begin to melt away.

Worry and anxiety are sand in the machinery of life; faith is the oil.
E. STANLEY JONES

A Prayer to Start Your Day

Father, sometimes troubles and distractions preoccupy my thoughts and trouble my soul. When I am anxious, Lord, let me turn my prayers to You. When I am worried, give me faith in You. Let me live courageously, dear God, knowing that You love me and that You will protect me, today and forever. Amen.

Love According to God

This is My commandment,
that you love one another as I have loved you.
JOHN 15:12 NKJV

You know the profound love that you hold in your heart for your own family and friends. As a child of God, you can only imagine the infinite love that your heavenly Father holds for you. So what, precisely, will you do in response to the Creator's love? Will you ignore it or embrace it? Will you return it or neglect it? That decision, of course, is yours and yours alone.

When you embrace God's love, your life's purpose is forever changed. When you embrace God's love, you feel differently about yourself, your neighbors, your family, and your world. More importantly, you share God's message—and His love—with others.

Your heavenly Father—a God of infinite love and mercy—is always reaching out to you. Accept His love, and share it. Love today, tomorrow, and forever.

The best use of life is love. The best expression
of love is time. The best time to love is now.
RICK WARREN

A Prayer to Start Your Day

Dear Lord, You have given me the gift of love; let me share that gift with others. And keep me mindful that the essence of love is not to receive it, but to give it, today and forever. Amen.

Choose Wisely, Worry Less

I have set before you life and death, blessing and curse.
Choose life so that you and your descendants may live,
love the LORD your God, obey Him, and remain faithful to Him.
For He is your life, and He will prolong your life in the land
the LORD swore to give to your fathers Abraham, Isaac, and Jacob.

DEUTERONOMY 30:19–20 HCSB

Life is a series of decisions and choices. Each day, we make countless decisions that can bring us closer to God, or not. When we live according to God's commandments, we earn for ourselves the abundance and peace that He intends for our lives. But if we become distracted and stray from His path, we create worries for ourselves and our families.

Do you seek spiritual abundance that can be yours through the person of God's only begotten Son? Then invite Christ into your heart and live according to His teachings. And when you confront a difficult decision or a powerful temptation, seek God's wisdom and trust it. When you do, you will receive untold blessings—not only for this day, but also for all eternity.

At the fork in every road, choose the road
that brings you nearer to God.

ELIZABETH GEORGE

A Prayer to Start Your Day

Heavenly Father, I have many choices to make. Help me choose wisely and worry less as I follow in the footsteps of Your only begotten Son. Amen.

Keep Praying
and Keep Growing

Like newborn infants, desire the pure spiritual milk,
so that you may grow by it for your salvation.
1 PETER 2:2 HCSB

When will you be a "fully grown" Christian? Never—or at least not until you arrive in heaven! As a believer living here on planet earth, you're never "fully grown"; you always have the potential to keep growing.

In those quiet moments when you open your heart to God, the One who made you keeps remaking you. He gives you direction, perspective, wisdom, and courage.

Would you like a time-tested formula for spiritual growth? Here it is: Keep studying God's Word, keep obeying His commandments, Keep praying (and listening for answers), and keep trying to live in the center of God's will. When you do, you'll never stay stuck for long. You will, instead, be a growing Christian, and that's precisely the kind of Christian God wants you to be.

Grow, dear friends, but grow, I beseech you,
in God's way, which is the only true way.
HANNAH WHITALL SMITH

A Prayer to Start Your Day

Dear Lord, thank You for the opportunity to walk with Your Son. And thank You for the opportunity to grow closer to You each day. I thank You for the person I am . . . and for the person You are growing me to be. Amen.

Beware of Keeping Up Appearances

*For am I now trying to win the favor of people, or God?
Or am I striving to please people? If I were still trying
to please people, I would not be a slave of Christ.*

GALATIANS 1:10 HCSB

Are you worried about keeping up appearances? Do you spend too much time, energy, or money on things that make you look good? If so, you are certainly not alone. Ours is a society that focuses upon appearances. We are told that we can't be "too thin or too rich." But in truth, the important things in life have little to do with fashion, fame, or fortune.

Today spend less time trying to please the world and more time trying to please your earthly family and your Father in heaven. Focus on pleasing your God and your loved ones, and don't worry about trying to impress the folks you happen to pass on the street. It takes too much energy—and too much life—to keep up appearances. So don't waste your energy.

*Outside appearances, things like the clothes you wear
or the car you drive, are important to other people
but totally unimportant to God. Trust God.*

MARIE T. FREEMAN

A Prayer to Start Your Day

Dear Lord, the world focuses on my outward appearance, but You see my heart. Today, Father, I will guard my heart as I focus upon the real person I am today and the person I can become tomorrow. Amen.

Trust God's Timetable

He has made everything appropriate in its time.
He has also put eternity in their hearts, but man cannot
discover the work God has done from beginning to end.

ECCLESIASTES 3:11 HCSB

If you want to trust God's plan for your life, then you must learn to trust His timetable. You will be sorely tempted, however, to do otherwise. Because you are a fallible human being, you are impatient for things to happen. But God knows best.

God has created a world that unfolds according to His own timetable, not ours . . . thank goodness! We mortals might make a terrible mess of things. God does not.

God's plan does not always happen in the way that we would like or at the time of our own choosing. Our task—as believing Christians who trust in a benevolent, all-knowing Father—is to wait patiently for God to reveal Himself. And reveal Himself He will. Always. But until God's perfect plan is made known, we must walk in faith and never lose hope. And we must continue to trust Him. Always.

We must learn to move according to the timetable
of the Timeless One, and to be at peace.

ELISABETH ELLIOT

A Prayer to Start Your Day

Dear Lord, Your timing is seldom my timing, but Your timing is always right for me. When I am impatient, remind me that You are never early or late. You are always on time, Lord, so let me trust in You today and every day. Amen.

You Don't Have to Be Perfect

Those who wait for perfect weather will never plant seeds;
those who look at every cloud will never harvest crops.
ECCLESIASTES 11:4 NCV

Expectations, expectations, expectations! As a citizen of the twenty-first-century world, you know that demands can be high, and expectations even higher. The media delivers an endless stream of messages that tell you how to look, how to behave, how to eat, and how to dress. The media's expectations are impossible to meet—God's are not. God doesn't expect you to be perfect, and neither should you.

Remember: the expectations that really matter are God's expectations. Everything else is inconsequential by comparison. So do your best to please God, and don't worry too much about what other people think. And when it comes to meeting the unrealistic expectations of our media-driven world, forget about trying to be perfect—it's impossible.

If it's your goal to always be right in everything, your soul will suffer.
ST. THÉRÈSE OF LISIEUX

A Prayer to Start Your Day

Lord, this world has so many expectations of me, but today I will not seek to meet those; I will do my best to meet Your expectations. I will make You my ultimate priority, Lord, by serving You, by praising You, by loving You, and by obeying You. Amen.

Fear Not: You Are Protected

*Even when I go through the darkest valley,
I fear no danger, for You are with me.*
PSALM 23:4 HCSB

A terrible storm rose quickly on the Sea of Galilee, and the disciples were afraid. Although they had witnessed many miracles, the disciples feared for their lives, so they turned to Jesus, and He calmed the waters and the wind.

Sometimes we, like Jesus's disciples, feel threatened by the storms of life. When we are fearful, we, too, should turn to Him for comfort and for courage.

The next time you find yourself facing a fear-provoking situation, remember that the One who calmed the wind and the waves is also your personal Savior. Then ask yourself which is stronger: your faith or your fear. The answer should be obvious. So when the storm clouds form overhead and you find yourself being tossed on the stormy seas of life, remember this: Wherever you are, God is there too. And because He cares for you, you are protected.

*In my experience, God rarely makes our fear disappear.
Instead, He asks us to be strong and take courage.*
BRUCE WILKINSON

A Prayer to Start Your Day

Dear Lord, when I am fearful, keep me mindful that You are my protector and my salvation. Thank You, Father, for a perfect love that casts out fear. Because of You, I can live courageously and faithfully this day and every day. Amen.

Grow in Your Relationship with Jesus

But whoever keeps His word, truly in him the love of God is perfected. This is how we know we are in Him: The one who says he remains in Him should walk just as He walked.

1 JOHN 2:5-6 HCSB

Who's the best friend this world has ever had? Jesus, of course. And when you form a life-changing relationship with Him, He will be your best friend too. And He will be your friend forever.

Jesus has offered to share the gifts of everlasting life and everlasting love with the world and with you. If you make mistakes, He'll stand by you. If you fall short of His commandments, He'll still love you. If you feel lonely or worried, He can touch your heart and lift your spirits.

Jesus wants you to enjoy a happy, healthy, abundant life. He wants you to walk with Him and to share His Good News. You can do it. And with a friend like Jesus, you will.

The crucial question for each of us is this: What do you think of Jesus, and do you yet have a personal acquaintance with Him?

HANNAH WHITALL SMITH

A Prayer to Start Your Day

Thank You, Lord, for Your Son. Today I will count Him as my dearest friend, and I will share His transforming message with a world in desperate need of His peace. Amen.

Find the Right Path

*Then He said to them all, "If anyone wants to come with Me,
he must deny himself, take up his cross daily, and follow Me."*
LUKE 9:23 HCSB

When we genuinely turn our hearts toward the face of God, we feel the sense that He is inviting us to walk with Him. And that's precisely the path that we must follow.

When we behave ourselves as faithful servants, we honor the Father and the Son. And when we live righteously and according to God's commandments, He blesses us in ways that we cannot fully understand.

So as this day unfolds, take every step of your journey with God as your traveling companion. Study His holy Word. Follow His commandments. Support only those activities that further God's kingdom and your spiritual growth. Be an example of righteous living to your friends, to your neighbors, and to your children. Then reap the blessings that God has promised to all those who accept His invitation of life abundant and life eternal.

*Walk in the daylight of God's will because
then you will be safe; you will not stumble.*
ANNE GRAHAM LOTZ

A Prayer to Start Your Day

Lord, sometimes life is difficult. But even when I can't see any hope for the future, You are always with me. And I can live courageously because I know that Your path leads me to a place where I can accomplish Your kingdom's work. Where You lead, I will follow. Amen.

85

Stay Focused on the Right Things

This day—and every day hereafter—is a chance to celebrate the life that God has given you. It's also a chance to give thanks to the One who has offered you more blessings than you can possibly count. What is your focus today? Are you willing to focus your thoughts on God's blessings and upon His will for your life? Or will you turn your thoughts to other things?

Today why not focus your thoughts on the joy that is rightfully yours in Christ? Why not take time to celebrate God's glorious creation? Why not trust your hopes instead of your fears? When you do, you will think optimistically about yourself and your world, and you can then share your optimism with others. They'll be better for it, and so will you. But not necessarily in that order.

A Prayer to Start Your Day

Dear Lord, help me to face this day with a spirit of optimism and thanksgiving. And let me focus my thoughts on You and Your incomparable gifts. Amen.

86

Trust God's Will

The Lord has a plan for our world and for our lives. God does not do things by accident; He has a perfect plan for His creation, a plan that includes each of us. But because we are mortal beings with limited understanding, we can never fully comprehend the will of God. No matter. As believers in a benevolent heavenly Father, we must always trust the will of God, even though we cannot fully understand it.

As this day unfolds, seek God's will and obey His Word. When you entrust your life to Him completely, He will give you strength to meet any challenge, courage to face any trial, and the wisdom to live in His righteousness and in His peace.

A Prayer to Start Your Day

Lord, let Your will be my will. When I am confused, give me maturity and wisdom. When I am worried, give me courage and strength. Let me be Your faithful servant, Father, always trusting Your guidance and Your will for my life. Amen.

87

Be Thankful

Each of us has much to be thankful for. We all have more blessings than we can count, beginning with the precious gift of life. Every good gift comes from our Father above, and we owe Him our never-ending thanks. But sometimes, when the demands of everyday life press down upon us, we neglect to express our gratitude to the Creator.

God loves us; He cares for us; He has a plan for each of us; and, He has offered us the gift of eternal life through His Son. Considering all the things that the Lord has done, we owe it to Him—and to ourselves—to slow down each day and offer our thanks. His grace is everlasting; our thanks should be too.

A Prayer to Start Your Day

Heavenly Father, Your gifts are greater than I can imagine. May I live each day with thanksgiving in my heart and praise on my lips. Thank You for the gift of Your Son and for the promise of eternal life. Let me share the joyous news of Jesus Christ, and let my life be a testimony to His love and His grace. Amen.

88

Praise Him

Enter his gates with thanksgiving and his courts with praise;
give thanks to him and praise his name.

PSALM 100:4 NIV

Because of God's promises, we must never lose hope in the priceless gifts of eternal love and eternal life. And because we are so richly blessed, we must approach our heavenly Father with reverence and praise and thanksgiving.

Sometimes in our rush "to get things done," we simply don't stop long enough to pause and praise our Creator for the countless blessings He has bestowed upon us. But when we slow down and express our gratitude to the One who made us, we enrich our own lives and the lives of those around us.

Thankful praise should become a habit, a regular part of our daily routines. God has blessed us beyond measure, and we owe Him everything, including our eternal praise. Let us praise Him today, tomorrow, and throughout eternity.

Praising God reduces your cares, levels your anxieties,
and multiplies your blessings.

SUZANNE DALE EZELL

A Prayer to Start Your Day

Dear Lord, today and every day I will praise You. I will come to You with hope in my heart and words of gratitude on my lips. Let me follow in the footsteps of Your Son, and let my thoughts, my prayers, my words, and my deeds praise You now and forever. Amen.

89

Are You Too Busy?

Be careful not to forget the LORD.
DEUTERONOMY 6:12 HCSB

Has the busy pace of life robbed you of the peace and contentment that you believe are rightfully yours? Do you have too many obligations and too few hours in which to get them done? If so, you are simply too busy for your own good. Through His Son, God offers you a peace that passes human understanding, but He won't force His peace upon you. In order to experience His peace, you must slow down long enough to sense His presence and be reminded of His promises.

Today, as a gift to yourself, to your family, and to the world, slow down, calm down, quiet yourself, and claim the inner peace that is your spiritual birthright: the peace of Jesus Christ. His peace, like His love, is offered freely. And the rest is up to you.

You cannot afford to be too busy to pray.
BILLY GRAHAM

A Prayer to Start Your Day

Dear Lord, when the quickening pace of life leaves me with little time for worship or for praise, help me to reorder my priorities. When the demands of the day leave me distracted and discouraged, let me turn to Jesus for the peace that only He can give. And then, when I have accepted the spiritual abundance that is mine through Christ, let me share His love with all who cross my path. Amen.

Begin Problem-Solving 101

*People who do what is right may have many problems,
but the LORD will solve them all.*

PSALM 34:19 NCV

Face facts: The upcoming day will not be problem-free. In fact, your life can be viewed as an exercise in problem solving. The question is not whether you will encounter problems; the real question is how you will choose to address them.

When it comes to solving the problems of everyday living, we often know precisely what needs to be done, but we may be slow in doing it—especially if what needs to be done is difficult or uncomfortable. So we put off till tomorrow what should be done today.

The words of Psalm 34 remind us that the Lord solves problems for "people who do what is right." And usually, doing "what is right" means doing the uncomfortable work of confronting our problems sooner rather than later. So with no further ado, let the problem solving begin . . . *now.*

Let God's promises shine on your problems.

CORRIE TEN BOOM

A Prayer to Start Your Day

Dear heavenly Father, when I am troubled, You heal me. When I am afraid, You protect me. When I am discouraged, You lift me up. In times of adversity, let me trust Your plan for my life. And whatever my circumstances, Lord, let me always give the thanks and the glory to You. Amen.

Put Faith above Feelings

Now the just shall live by faith.
HEBREWS 10:38 NKJV

Who is in charge of your emotions? Is it you, or have you formed the unfortunate habit of letting other people—or troubling situations—determine the quality of your thoughts and the direction of your day? If you're wise, and if you'd like to build a better life for yourself and your loved ones, you'll learn to control your emotions before your emotions control you.

Human emotions are highly variable, decidedly unpredictable, and often unreliable. Our emotions are like the weather, only far more fickle. So we must learn to live by faith, not by the ups and downs of our own emotional roller coasters.

Sometime during this day, you will probably be gripped by a strong negative feeling. Distrust it. Rein it in. Test it. And turn it over to God. Your emotions will inevitably change; God will not. So trust Him completely as you watch those negative feelings slowly evaporate into thin air—which, of course, they will.

*Our emotions can lie to us, and we need
to counter our emotions with truth.*
BILLY GRAHAM

A Prayer to Start Your Day

Heavenly Father, You are my strength and my refuge. As I journey through this day, I will encounter events that cause me emotional distress. Lord, when I am troubled, let me turn to You. Keep me steady, Lord, and in those difficult moments, renew a right spirit inside my heart. Amen.

Make God's Priorities Your Priorities

Draw near to God, and He will draw near to you.
JAMES 4:8 HCSB

Have you fervently asked God to help prioritize Your life? Have you asked Him for guidance and for the courage to do the things that you know need to be done? If so, then you're continually inviting your Creator to reveal Himself in a variety of ways. As a follower of Christ, you must do no less.

When you make God's priorities your priorities, you will receive God's abundance and His peace. When you make God a full partner in every aspect of your life, He will lead you along the proper path: His path. When you allow God to reign over your heart, He will honor you with spiritual blessings that are simply too numerous to count. So as you plan for the day ahead, make God's will your ultimate priority. When you do, every other priority will have a tendency to fall neatly into place.

The whole point of getting things done
is knowing what to leave undone.
OSWALD CHAMBERS

A Prayer to Start Your Day

Lord, let Your priorities be my priorities. Let Your will be my will. Let Your Word be my guide, and let me grow in faith and in wisdom this day and every day. Amen.

He's Right Here, Right Now

The LORD is with you when you are with Him.
If you seek Him, He will be found by you.
2 CHRONICLES 15:2 HCSB

Since God is everywhere, we are free to sense His presence whenever we take the time to quiet our souls and turn our prayers to Him. But sometimes, amid the incessant demands of everyday life, we turn our thoughts far from God; when we do, we suffer.

Do you set aside quiet moments each day to offer praise to your Creator? Silence is a gift that you give to yourself and to God. During these moments of stillness, you will often sense the infinite love and power of your Creator—and He, in turn, will speak directly to your heart.

The familiar words of Psalm 46:10 remind us to "be still, and know that I am God" ((NIV). When we do so, we encounter the awesome presence of our loving heavenly Father, and we are comforted in the knowledge that God is not just near. He is here.

Mark it down. You will never go where God is not.
MAX LUCADO

A Prayer to Start Your Day

Heavenly Father, help me to feel Your presence in every situation and every circumstance. You are with me, Lord, in times of celebration and in times of sorrow. You are with me when I am strong and when I am weak. Today let me experience Your presence so that others, too, might know You through me. Amen.

Be Strong and Courageous

Be strong and courageous, and do the work.
Don't be afraid or discouraged, for the LORD God, my God,
is with you. He won't leave you or forsake you.
1 CHRONICLES 28:20 HCSB

Life can be difficult and discouraging at times. During our darkest moments, we can depend upon our friends and family, and upon God. When we do, we find the courage to face even the darkest days with hopeful hearts and willing hands.

Eleanor Roosevelt advised, "You gain strength, courage, and confidence by every great experience in which you really stop to look fear in the face. You are able to say to yourself, 'I lived through this horror. I can take the next thing that comes along.' You must do the thing you think you cannot do."

So the next time you find your courage tested to the limit, remember that you're probably stronger than you think. And remember that with you, your friends, your family, and your God all working together, you have nothing to fear.

What is courage? It is the ability to be strong in trust,
in conviction, in obedience. To be courageous is to step
out in faith—to trust and obey, no matter what.
KAY ARTHUR

A Prayer to Start Your Day

Dear Lord, fill me with Your Spirit and help me face my challenges with courage and determination. Keep me mindful, Father, that You are with me always, and with You by my side, I have nothing to fear. Amen.

Obey Now

Not everyone who says to Me, "Lord, Lord!" will enter the kingdom of heaven, but only the one who does the will of My Father in heaven.

MATTHEW 7:21 HCSB

God's laws are eternal and unchanging: obedience leads to abundance and joy; disobedience leads to disaster. God has given us a guidebook for righteous living called the Holy Bible. If we trust God's Word and live by it, we are blessed. But if we choose to ignore God's commandments, the results are as predictable as they are tragic.

Each day, we make countless decisions that can bring us closer to God, or not. Do you seek God's peace and His blessings? Then obey Him. When you're faced with a difficult choice or a powerful temptation, seek God's counsel and obey the counsel He gives. Invite God into your heart and live according to His commandments. When you do, you will be blessed today and tomorrow and forever.

Obedience is a foundational stepping-stone on the path of God's will.

ELIZABETH GEORGE

A Prayer to Start Your Day

Dear Lord, let me live according to Your commandments. Direct my path far from the temptations and distractions of this world. And, let me discover Your will and obey it, Lord, this day and always. Amen.

Tackle Tough Times

God is our refuge and strength, a very present help in trouble.
PSALM 46:1 NKJV

Christians of every generation have experienced adversity, and this generation is no different. But today's Christians face challenges that previous generations could have scarcely imagined. Although the world continues to change, God's love remains constant. And He remains ready to comfort us and strengthen us whenever we turn to Him.

Where is the best place to take your worries? Take them to God. Take your troubles to Him; take your fears to Him; take your doubts to Him; take your weaknesses to Him; take your frustrations to Him, and leave them all there. Seek protection from the One who offers you eternal salvation; build your spiritual house upon the Rock that cannot be moved. Then, perhaps, you will worry less and trust God more, and that's as it should be because God is trustworthy, and you are protected.

Don't let obstacles along the road to eternity
shake your confidence in God's promises.
DAVID JEREMIAH

A Prayer to Start Your Day

Dear heavenly Father, when I am fearful, You give me courage. You are my source of strength, and my shield. Even when I encounter tough times, I trust Your plan for my life. And whatever my circumstances, Lord, I will offer praise and thanks to You. Amen.

Pray Specifically

*Rejoice always! Pray constantly. Give thanks in everything,
for this is God's will for you in Christ Jesus.*

1 THESSALONIANS 5:16–18 HCSB

As the old saying goes, if it's big enough to worry about, it's big enough to pray about. Yet sometimes we don't pray about the specific details of our lives. Instead, we may offer general prayers that are decidedly heavy on platitudes and decidedly light on particulars.

The next time you pray, try this: Be very specific about the things you ask God to do. Of course God already knows precisely what you need—He knows infinitely more about your life than you do—but you need the experience of talking to your Creator in honest, unambiguous language.

So today don't be vague with God. Tell Him exactly what you need. He doesn't need to hear the details, but you do.

*God says we don't need to be anxious about anything;
we just need to pray about everything.*

STORMIE OMARTIAN

A Prayer to Start Your Day

Dear Lord, today and every day, I will seek Your guidance and listen for Your instructions. I will come to You in prayer, Father, and when I do, I will trust Your answers. Amen.

Claim Lasting Peace

Be of good comfort, be of one mind, live in peace;
and the God of love and peace will be with you.
2 CORINTHIANS 13:11 NKJV

The beautiful words of John 14:27 promise that Jesus offers peace: "Peace I leave with you. My peace I give to you. I do not give to you as the world gives. Your heart must not be troubled or fearful" (HCSB). Your challenge is to accept Christ's peace into your heart and then, as best you can, to share His peace with your neighbors. But sometimes that's easier said than done.

If you are a person with lots of obligations and responsibilities, it is a fact of life: You worry. From time to time, you worry about finances, safety, health, home, family, and countless other concerns. Where is the best place to take your worries? Take them to God, and leave them there.

Today, as a gift to yourself, to your family, and to your friends, claim the inner peace that is your spiritual birthright: the peace of Jesus Christ. Christ is standing at the door, waiting patiently for you to invite Him to reign over your heart. His eternal peace is offered freely. Claim it today.

Emotional peace and calm come after doing God's will and not before.
ERWIN LUTZER

A Prayer to Start Your Day

Dear Lord, let me claim the peace and abundance that You offer through Your Son, Jesus. You are the Giver of all things good, Father, and You give me peace when I draw close to You. Help me to trust Your will, to follow Your commands, and to accept Your peace, today and forever. Amen.

Live on Purpose

*Therefore I, the prisoner for the Lord,
urge you to walk worthy of the calling you have received.*
EPHESIANS 4:1 HCSB

What does God intend for me to do with my life?" It's an easy question to ask but, for many of us, a difficult question to answer. Why? Because God's purposes aren't always clear to us. Sometimes we wander aimlessly in a wilderness of our own making. And sometimes we struggle mightily against God in an unsuccessful attempt to find success and happiness through our own means, not His.

If you sincerely seek God's guidance, He will give it. But be forewarned: He will make His revelations known to you in a way and in a time of His choosing, not yours. So be patient.

Today and every day, God is beckoning you to hear His voice and follow His purpose for your life. When you listen carefully—and patiently—you'll be amazed at the wonderful things that an all-knowing, all-powerful God can do

*God will help us become the people
we are meant to be, if only we will ask Him.*
HANNAH WHITALL SMITH

A Prayer to Start Your Day

Dear Lord, I know that You have a purpose for my life, and I will seek that purpose today and every day that I live. Let my actions be pleasing to You, and let me share Your Good News with a world that so desperately needs Your healing hand and the salvation of Your Son. Amen.

100

Make the Ultimate Choice

For God so loved the world that He gave His only begotten Son, that whoever believes in Him should not perish but have everlasting life.

JOHN 3:16 NKJV

Jesus is not only the light of the world; He is also its salvation. He came to this earth so that we might not perish, but instead spend eternity with Him. What a glorious gift; what a priceless opportunity.

As mere mortals, we cannot fully understand the scope, and thus the value, of eternal life. Our vision is limited but God's is not. He sees all things; He knows all things; and His plans for you extend throughout eternity.

If you haven't already done so, this is the perfect moment to make the ultimate choice and turn your life over to God's only begotten Son. When you give your heart to the Son, you belong to the Father—today, tomorrow, and for all eternity.

*Jesus became mortal to give you immortality;
and today, through Him, you can be free.*

DAVID JEREMIAH

A Prayer to Start Your Day

I know, Lord, that this world is not my home because You have given me the priceless gift of eternal life through Your Son Jesus. Keep the hope of heaven fresh in my heart, and, while I am in this world, help me to pass through it with faith in my heart and praise on my lips . . . for You. Amen.